SHORT CUTS

INTRODUCTIONS TO FILM STUDIES

HERITAGE FILM

NATION, GENRE AND REPRESENTATION

BELÉN VIDAL

WALLFLOWER

LONDON and NEW YORK

A Wallflower Book
Published by
Columbia University Press
Publishers Since 1893
New York • Chichester, West Sussex
cup.columbia.edu

A complete CIP record is available from the Library of Congress

ISBN 978-0-231-16203-6 (pbk. : alk. paper)
ISBN 978-0-231-85004-9 (e-book)

Columbia University Press books are printed on permanent and durable acid-free paper.
This book is printed on paper with recycled content.

Printed in the United States of America

p 10 9 8 7 6 5 4 3 2 1

CONTENTS

ACKNOWLEDGEMENTS

I would like to thank the Carnegie Trust for the Universities of Scotland for its financial support towards the publication of this book. Huge thanks too to Yoram Allon at Wallflower Press for the opportunity and his patience at the various times when life and chance interfered with the progress of the work.

I am indebted to my colleagues in the department of Film Studies at King's College London for offering the nurturing intellectual environment and day-to-day support that have made possible for me to complete this book.

This volume also owes a debt to friends and colleagues in various institutions. Our conversations over the years provided inspiration and greatly enriched my understanding of the issues at stake; especially John Caughie (who made me realise how crucial television was to the heritage film), Julianne Pidduck, David Martin-Jones, Mette Hjort, William Brown and Yun Mi Hwang. In addition, I would like to thank my MLitt/MA students at both the University of St Andrews and King's College London for stimulating discussions around the heritage film.

Very special thanks are due to Ginette Vincendeau and Gary Needham for reading and commenting on sections of the manuscript, but also for their continuous encouragement and friendly support. Jen Rutherford greatly helped improve the final draft with her sharp proofreading, giving generous assistance when it was most needed. Any errors and infelicities that may remain in the book are entirely my own.

Finally, I would like to express my deep gratitude to Manuel Pérez Carballo, for being there every step of the (long) way with love and humour, for watching and talking for hours on end.

INTRODUCTION: PLACING THE HERITAGE FILM

Fans of the costume drama, audiences interested in films about historical characters and events, and even film students learning about history
and film may not recognise the term 'heritage film' immediately. Unlike
the western, the romantic comedy or the horror film, the heritage film is
not a genre in the industrial sense of the term. Rather, the concept has its
roots in British film studies, where it has become associated with a powerful undercurrent of nostalgia for the past conveyed by historical dramas,
romantic costume films and literary adaptations. These films often flaunt
their connections with classical works of the literary canon, lavish production values and star performances. They regularly stand up for prizes in
festivals and award ceremonies. They screen at both art cinemas and mul-
tiplexes, often as quality pictures, or at the mainstream end of the international art-film circuit. The heritage film is, in short, a distinctive strand
in contemporary cinema, albeit one dogged by a certain bad press. The
heritage film is often associated with craftsmanship, with competent yet
unexciting filmmaking. However, its complex links with issues of history
and representation, its continuous popularity and its relevance for the
study of the national cinemas warrant its critical interest; as we shall see,
its relation with the past – as well as with its own generic past – is anything
but static.

   This book examines the heritage film in light of the critical debates that
have shaped its reception. Throughout the book, the term 'heritage film'
co-exists with the more strongly generic 'period film' and 'costume film' (or
'costume drama'). All terms convey a type of film that places its characters
in a recognisable moment of the past, enhanced by the mise-en-scène of
historical reconstruction. The focus on fictional characters, romantic plots
and period spectacle often situates this genre outside the domain staked

by the historical film (see Grindon 1994; Sargeant 2000; Chapman 2005; Burgoyne 2008). However, the films examined in this book under the umbrella term of heritage cinema share the historical film's 'dual focus', what Robert Burgoyne defines as 'the juxtaposition of the old and the new, the powerful sense that what is being rendered on-screen is not an imaginary world, but a once-existing world that is being reinscribed in an original way' (2008: 11). The heritage film's simultaneous investment in authenticity as well as reinterpretation reflects its time and place in film history.

This book explores the heritage film as a flexible critical category that addresses trends in production, narrative and representation within a particular time-frame: the period comprised between the 1980s and the end of the 2000s. Particular attention is given to the emergence and impact of the debates that introduced the term into film studies; the heritage film debate is a modern critical development that follows the re-emergence of the period film in the late 1970s. As François de la Bretèque has noted (1992: 113), although the period film is a staple genre of popular cinemas, it was only at the end of the 'new waves', with their almost exclusive focus on the present, that European art cinemas resumed their interest in filming the past. In Britain, where the term heritage film first gained critical currency, films such as *Chariots of Fire* (Hugh Hudson, 1981) ignited a debate about the relationship between these fictions about the past and the competing representations of the nation vying for attention in 1980s British cinema. This context gave the original debates a markedly political slant but also brought to the fore key questions about realism and the middlebrow that continue to inform the study of British cinema (and television) today.

The heritage film thus needs to be considered as a 'critically or theoretically constructed genre' rather than an industrial one (Neale 1990: 52). The heritage film debate connects the period film to a network of cultural and industrial practices that relate to the construction of a collective cultural memory. This phenomenon is not exclusive to the British film industry. Scholarly discussion of the heritage film has taken root in contexts as different as France, where there has been a turn to the study of so-called *fictions patrimoniales* (see Moine and Beylot 2009), or South Korea, with emergent English-language scholarship on *sageuk* or historical drama (see Chung 2008; Hwang 2011). The term heritage film has also been mapped, with different emphases, onto the Italian, Spanish, German, Polish, Scandinavian, Australian, Thai and North American contexts, among others. This indicates not only the international scope of the genre but also the increasing internationalisation of this paradigm in film studies. The heritage film thus has become a supple term to refer to the ways in which national cinemas turn to the past at different moments in their histories in search of their own foundational myths. At the same time the genre also highlights the strategic positioning of national film industries in the global markets and their need for expansion through transnational alliances.

The latter aspect is of particular relevance for this book, which examines the internationalisation of the heritage film from the perspective of British and European cinemas. There are several reasons for this. First and foremost, this book aims to provide an introduction to the foundational arguments that developed during the first two decades (1990–2010) of English-language studies on the heritage film. In this respect, the book's departure point is a set of debates that are specific to British cinema (even if the genre and modes of filmmaking identified by such debates are not).

Secondly, I am also attentive to the gains and losses that derive from the circulation of national cinemas in international contexts. The heritage film touches areas of cultural anxiety about issues of identity politics, appropriation and misrepresentation, all the more marked in film nations shaped by heritages of colonial domination and post-colonial self-determination. I am therefore wary of extending further a framework of study linked to European contexts of production and circulation (even if, as Thomas Elsaesser has claimed (2005), contemporary European cinema should perhaps be redefined as a subset of world cinema, rather than as its Other). Whereas the study of the heritage film in Asian contexts, for example, constitutes an exciting development, a film like *Joseon namnyeo sangyeoljisa* (*Untold Scandal*, Je-yong Lee, 2003), a South Korean period drama inspired by the French literary classic *Dangerous Liaisons*, also raises a whole new set of questions regarding transculturation that go beyond the limited scope of this book.

Thirdly, the book uses the discussion of the heritage film as an opportunity to reconnect British cinema to its European context. This occurs, regrettably, at the cost of losing focus on the particular articulation of Scottish, Welsh as well Irish heritage cinemas. Their separate histories challenge the very notion of a British heritage film that, as it has been often noted by its critics, tends to make the iconography of Englishness the norm. Accordingly, the inclusion of a central chapter that interrogates the existence of the heritage film as a European genre responds to my own desire, as a non-British film studies scholar watching films in Britain, to contribute to an ongoing discussion involving specialists who view British cinema from Europe, or turn towards Europe through the looking glass of British cinema.[1]

This approach will hopefully contribute to illuminate the heritage film's fluid position in a map of exchanges and influences in which, as it has often been noted, it stands alongside auteur cinema as the most exportable European genre. Reframing the British film as a European phenomenon also helps explain the economic and institutional developments that inform its narratives and aesthetics, including contact with and assimilation to a decentralised, worldwide Hollywood. Last but not least, this book is particularly interested in stretching, reworking and updating a concept that is constantly reconfiguring its generic borders, and in pointing at potential areas for further critical expansion. It is my contention that the heritage film is a hybrid genre with porous borders, a genre that is becoming less consensual and more political through its own staunch preference for emotional histories, and also more adventurous in its continuous incorporation of a popular historical iconography informed not only by literature or painting, but also by fashion, popular music and television.

Chapter 1 examines the uses of the term 'heritage film' in its original contexts. The success of British costume films and television dramas in the 1980s made these period fictions the object of intense academic debates over the transformation of the national past into a cultural commodity. The British heritage film was singled out for its conservative aesthetic that revelled in a reassuring iconography of English tradition characterised by pastoral, upper-class lifestyles and a largely uncritical use of images of empire. These films about the past were linked to a nostalgic desire to escape from a present marked by socio-economic crisis in 1980s Britain. The chapter examines these debates in connection with traditions of quality, ongoing questions about the middlebrow in British cinema, and the interaction between the film and television industries, which has defined the key role of the heritage film in British film culture. The chapter closes with a study of *The Queen* (Stephen Frears, 2006) a British monarchy film that signals the continuing presence of the historical past in the contemporary popular imagination.

Chapter 2 focuses on the production cycles and cultural significance of the heritage film within and beyond the British context. As the term ventures into other national cinemas the heritage film can be claimed as a characteristic genre in various European film traditions. The heritage film is explored in relation to state intervention in the European context and top-down institutional approaches that shape official discourses of national identity. Whether this amounts to the existence of such a thing as a 'European heritage film' is debatable. Instead, through a wide selection of examples the chapter interrogates the ways in which the heritage film may contribute to the rebranding of European cinemas in the international markets. This rebranding needs to be understood with regard to supra-national production frameworks (such as those supported by the European funding programmes MEDIA and Eurimages), new schemes of co-production, as well as in the increasing economic interdependence between Hollywood and Europe. This economic configuration underpins the heritage film's preoccupation with issues of national history and memory. The chapter looks at the multi-national production *Joyeux Noël* (*Merry Christmas*, Christian Carion, 2005) as an example of the above – a popular film that reflects the institutional move towards a notion of a European heritage built on a shared traumatic history.

Chapter 3 focuses on the aesthetics of the heritage film in relation to gender politics. This strand of the debate brings to the fore alternative representations of nation at a moment in which traditional assumptions about national cinemas are undergoing revision. The relevance of a gender critique for the analysis of the heritage film became evident after the crossover success of feminist art films *Orlando* (Sally Potter, 1992) and *The Piano* (Jane Campion, 1993). These films subvert the tenets of conventional realism and the tasteful aesthetics previously associated with heritage cinema. As such, they have been connected to a 'post-heritage' aesthetic. This line of criticism continues in relation to popular melodramas such as *The Duchess* (Saul Dibb, 2008), in which the ambiguous discourse on femininity and power expresses contemporary anxieties about consumption and celebrity cultures. The case study that concludes this chapter is *Girl with a Pearl Earring* (Peter Webber, 2003), which I examine in relation to the artist's biopic. This fictional story on an iconic artwork relocates the British heritage film into European settings in a narrative that shifts from the mystery of (masculine) genius to the reflection on feminine agency.

Finally, a brief note on the book's rationale. This book does not purport to be a comprehensive mapping of the genre. Instead, it seeks to put forward a methodological reflection about the heritage film as a film studies term. In order to achieve this I propose a selective guide to the debates, illustrated by the possibilities for analysis offered by the films themselves. This consideration informs the formal organisation of the book and the use of a majority of English-language examples (still the preferred language of most heritage co-productions that aspire to secure international distribution).

Note

1   The list includes Ian Christie, Pam Cook, Richard Dyer, Thomas Elsaesser, Geoffrey Nowell-Smith, Julianne Pidduck, Sarah Street, Ginette Vincendeau and Eckart Voigts-Virchow, among others.

1 THE BRITISH HERITAGE FILM: NATION AND REPRESENTATION

In 2007 the British television institution BBC (British Broadcasting Corporation) aired a seven-part series entitled 'British Film Forever' as part of a high-profile 'Summer of British Film' co-organised with the UK Film Council. The series combined an educational remit (raising the profile and celebrating the best of British cinema) with a popular edge. Rather than following a historical timeline highlighting key films and filmmakers, each episode of the series focused on one film genre and supported its narrative with a collage of excerpts from films from all periods, interspersed with interview snippets with critics and celebrities. This (necessarily selective) vision of British film history attracted some strong criticism.[1] However, the show condensed into an accessible argument some enduring polemics in British film studies and, in particular, the central role of costume drama to definitions of British film. The episode 'Corsets, Cleavage and Country Houses – The Story of Costume Drama' combined documentary footage of a 1980s Britain ravaged by conflict (riot police, unemployment, the miners' strike, the Falklands War) with idyllic countryside and tea-room scenes drawn from some of the most successful British costume dramas of that era. A tongue-in-cheek voice-over narration contrasted the two sets of radically different images with the captions: 'this was Britain in the 1980s' (the documentary footage) and 'this is what of the rest of the world thought we were up to' (the extracts from the costume films).

The BBC show's clear-cut opposition between an escapist cinema pitched to international (especially North American) 'heritage-hungry' tourism and the harsh socio-economic realities of life in Britain illustrates the normative force of the critical debates surrounding the so-called 'heritage film'. The series' presentation of the period film as a comforting antidote to unpalatable yet more urgent images of contemporary Britain is reminiscent of the distinction established by Thomas Elsaesser in 1993 between the projection of a complex 'social imaginary' of Britain, and a mythical 'national imaginary' – one for 'us' (the insider viewer) and one for 'them' (the international audiences). Such opposition highlights the 'Jekyll and Hyde' quality of British cinema as 'one of the orthodoxies of academic film studies' (Elsaesser 2006: 50, 54). This chapter investigates this orthodox discourse through a close look at the debates on the heritage film in the light of issues of myth and national identity, the tradition of quality in British film culture, and the convergence of cinema and television. These key threads provide the context for the analysis of the main case study, Stephen Frears' *The Queen*.

History versus heritage: a conservative mode of filmmaking?

The term heritage film gained critical currency with the international success of a set of British period dramas produced in the 1980s and early 1990s, including the historical films *Chariots of Fire* and *Gandhi* (Richard Attenborough, 1982) and film adaptations of E. M. Forster's novels: *A Passage To India* (David Lean, 1984), *A Room With a View* (James Ivory, 1986), *Maurice* (James Ivory, 1987), *Where Angels Fear to Tread* (Charles Sturridge, 1991) and *Howards End* (James Ivory, 1992). In 1993, an article by British film historian Andrew Higson, 'Re-presenting the National Past: Nostalgia and Pastiche in the Heritage Film' redefined this cycle of quality costume dramas as 'heritage films'. The heritage film has period settings (typically, Edwardian England or the British Raj), recurrent locations (the English countryside, Oxbridge, colonial India, Italy), slow-paced narratives that enhance character and the authenticity of period detail, and an opulent if static mise-en-scène exhibiting elaborate period costumes, artefacts, properties and heritage sites. The heritage film typically dwells on an iconography of upper-middle class and aristocratic privilege. For Higson, such iconography produces a highly selective vision of Englishness attached to pastoral and imperial values where the past as spectacle becomes the main attraction.

At the basis of this critique we find a tension between the surface of visual splendour and the liberal messages delivered by these character-centred dramas. Audiences are called upon to identify with the dilemmas experienced by characters under social pressure, yet the sumptuous recreation of bygone social milieus invites an appreciative look that undercuts the elements of social criticism. The representations of the past offered by the heritage film carry a glaring contradiction between form and narrative: 'the past is displayed as visually spectacular pastiche, inviting a nostalgic gaze that resists the ironies and social critiques so often suggested narratively by these films' (Higson 2006: 91). This becomes manifest in what Higson calls the production of 'heritage space': a pictorial film style that showcases sumptuous heritage sites and lavish décor, designed 'for the display of heritage properties rather than for the enactment of dramas' (2006: 99). Thus, architectural sites, interior designs, furnishings and, in general, the mise-en-scène of objects, settings and period artefacts become not just a conduit for narrative and characterisation but carry an ideological effect: they help construct a sense of Englishness according to a certain bourgeois ideal of imperial tradition, stability and propriety that belies the subtler ironies of the novels faithfully adapted. The heritage film would thus encourage a nostalgic look back to the certainties and the visual splendour of the national past.

Higson's critique put the spotlight on the films created by the partnership formed by American director James Ivory and Indian producer Ismail Merchant alongside their frequent collaborator, the German-born, English-educated writer of Polish-Jewish extraction Ruth Prawer Jhabvala. Their independent production company Merchant Ivory, founded in 1961, has distinguished itself through its cosmopolitan films. From its base in New York, Merchant Ivory has shot fiction films variously set in India, United States, England, France, China and Argentina. Throughout the 1960s, their efforts were focused on the production of Indian films shot in English and aimed at the international market, moving to a number of period and contemporary pieces with American themes in the 1970s and early 1980s (for instance, *The Bostonians*, James Ivory, 1984). However, their pre-1990s work has been eclipsed by the phenomenal success of their English period films, especially *A Room with a View, Howards End* and *The Remains of the Day* (James Ivory, 1993) which inserted Merchant Ivory into a tradition of tasteful literary adaptations and historical dramas in British cinema. Higson's critique of the heritage film highlights the 'Britishness' of Merchant Ivory's British films as a series of reductive images of 'Englishness' focused on the traditional values and lifestyles of the upper-middle classes and the aristocratic elite. Merchant Ivory's trademark emphasis on production values, classicist style and focus on the 'intimate observation of manners and unspoken desires' (Hall 2006) earned the company a reputation for quality, tasteful cinema. The internal conflicts that embattle the bourgeois households take place against the imposing background of wealthy country houses; their films recreate with anthropological zeal the fashions and objects of the periods in which the original novels were set. This selective vision of the British past was for some tantamount to the denial of the actual state of fragmentation of the social body, and of alternative versions of a plural national culture (see Corner & Harvey 1991).

Higson's critique transferred to the domain of film studies the discontent voiced by a section of journalists, historians and sociologists close to the political left, for whom the heritage film reflected the ideological construction of a 'national heritage' during Margaret Thatcher's years as British Primer Minister (1979–1990). Thatcher's conservative government imposed a top-down vision of heritage through policy (in particular, the National Heritage Acts of 1980 and 1983) and encouraged a culture of private enterprise, including the commerce with the signs and sites of the national past. The success of the cycle of 1980s period dramas coincided with the formation of an anti-heritage discourse (see Wright 1985 and Hewison 1987) which, as noted by Raphael Samuel, reacted against

Bourgeois interiors: Anthony Hopkins, Jemma Redgrave and Emma Thompson in *Howards End*

the historicist turn in British culture and the rise of the heritage industries (including the boom in historical tourism) at the onset of economic recession. Samuel describes the sentiment underpinning anti-heritage criticism in the following way:

> Heritage prepared the way for, or could be thought as giving expression to, a recrudescence of 'Little Englandism' and the revival of nationalism as a force in political life. It anticipated and gave expression to the triumph of Thatcherism in the sphere of high politics. Heritage, in short, was a symbol of national decadence; a malignant growth which testified at once to the strength of this country's *ancien régime* and to the weakness of radical alternatives to it. (1994: 261)

The critique of this new heritage culture was particularly trenchant with regard to the role played by film and television. In an early assessment of 1980s period drama Tana Wollen notes that the 'nostalgic screen fictions' produced around this time trade on their visual authenticity while co-opting collective memory to suit a conservative political agenda. What was at stake in the popularity of period drama was nothing less than the reconstruction of national identity based on a reactionary vision of the past (Wollen 1991).

These forceful ideological connotations co-exist with fascinating ambiguities of interpretation around the heritage film. The iconic *Chariots of Fire* is a case in point.[2] The film retrieves a forgotten episode of British sports history: the hard-won triumph of the British running team at the 1924 Olympic Games held in Paris. The film focuses on two keen athletes from different ethnic and class backgrounds, and on their individual stories of sacrifice and aspiration as well as their struggle against a reactionary establishment. Eric Liddell (Ian Charleson), a Scottish missionary born in China, is a fervent Sabbatarian who refuses to give up his religious principles for the sake of national pride. Harold Abrahams (Ben Cross), a Lithuanian Jew, struggles to overcome the ingrained racism of Cambridge University and hires Mussabini (Ian Holm), a professional coach of Italian and Arab descent, in an overt challenge to the amateur practice of sport, traditionally regarded as the preserve of the aristocracy. Lord Lindsay (Nigel Havers), the gentleman-sportsman and embodiment of aristocratic privilege, supports Abrahams and gallantly gives up his place in the 400 metres race in favour of Liddell. By relegating Lindsay to a supporting, enabling role and foregrounding Abrahams' victory as symbolic of his Englishness, *Chariots of Fire* reinforces the message that national identity and social status are 'honours that can be *earned*, not just acquired by inheritance' (Johnston 1985: 101; emphasis in original).

As perceptive analyses of the film point out (see Hill 1999, Chapman 2005) the multi-character narrative is sensitive to the complexities of national allegiance provoked by social exclusion and class privilege. However, the clash of modernity versus tradition that articulates the theme of individual achievement reverts to homogenous images of class, gender and nation that subsume the characters' differences within a dominant version of Englishness. The film's languorous mise-en-scène places its struggling heroes amidst imposing Cambridge University settings. In what is perhaps the best-remembered sequence in the film, Abrahams and Lindsay, surrounded by crowds of cheering students, honour the tradition of the college dash by racing around the Great Court in Trinity College.[3] The mise-en-scène momentarily infuses the ancient institution with youthful energy and dynamism, whilst cutaways to the masters of Caius and Trinity Colleges, who look down (literally and metaphorically) on Abrahams' racing exploits from a high window, intimate the hurdles that the Olympic hopeful will have to overcome. Abrahams' professional attitude towards sport is decidedly anti-establishment. However, the values espoused by the character link with the ideology of entrepeneurialism and competitiviness that also characterised Thatcherism (see Hill 1999).

The film as a whole similarly oscillates between the critique of traditional institutions and an elated celebration of fair play and male bonding that feeds into a conciliatory myth of an inclusive nation. As noted by Sheila Johnston, 'nationhood in *Chariots of Fire* is a dynamic thing, challenged by the interloper, yet remaining in essence unchanged' (1985: 104). Its central story of triumph over adversity is highlighted in the iconic sequence that bookends the film, in which all the protagonists, their class and cultural differences effaced by identical white running gear, train together on an open beach to a soaring theme by Vangelis. Their individual desires and aspirations, represented by their different running styles captured by medium close-ups that glide from one ecstatic face to the next, are reframed by long shots that create a romanticised vision of the group

Team spirit and individual stories: Harold Abrahams (Ben Cross) in *Chariots of Fire*

united in the collective effort. The use of non-diegetic electronic music and slow motion endows this idealised image of British masculinity with timeless poignancy. These stylistic flourishes upgrade a story in line with traditions of British realism and pre-1960s classical narrative style with an unmistakable 1980s pop-culture feel.

After a difficult financing process (the film eventually went ahead with backing from Twentieth Century-Fox and Allied Stars when Goldcrest producer David Puttnam failed to secure funding from British sources) *Chariots of Fire* opened in Britain to disappointing box-office figures. Yet its runaway success in the US, culminating at the 1982 Academy Awards (where it reaped four Oscars, including Best Film) facilitated a successful re-release in Britain later that year. *Chariots of Fire* triggered a period of confidence in the British film industry and British subject matter, which was subsumed within the Thatcherite discourse of patriotic values and entrepreneurism. The film's success became part of the triumphalist mood surrounding the British victory in the Falklands War. This context prompts Wollen to note that the film proposes patriotism as the 'resolution to social division and conflict' (1991: 182). For Leonard Quart (2006), the victory of the anti-establishment characters in favour of a dynamic and diverse nation is couched in an uncritical sentimentality that exults in nationalistic feeling, thereby implicitly endorsing the Thatcherite ethos. Such interpretations were emphatically resisted by the left-leaning Puttnam and scriptwriter

Colin Welland (Welland was a Labour Party activist and former collaborator of Ken Loach), who were dismayed at the government's attempt to capitalise on the success of *Chariots of Fire* as an opportunity for flag-waving propaganda (see Chapman 2005: 287). However, the film's strong iconicity and classical story of masculine achievement were easily appropriated by the political right. The praise bestowed on the film by both Thatcher and American president Ronald Reagan fits in with the transformation of Britain into a neo-capitalist nation of 'national brand names, company logos, icons and slogans: identity under the reign of "The Image"' (Elsaesser 2006: 49). In spite of its progressive message and leftist credentials, *Chariots of Fire* was mobilised as a vehicle to shore up support for New Conservatism on both sides of the Atlantic (see Johnston 1985).

The projection of a nostalgic, upper-class version of Englishness solidified into a national myth that found unparalleled success in the international image markets. This imaginary reinvention of the nation could be absorbed within the principles of enterprise and heritage enshrined by the successive Conservative governments of Thatcher and John Major (1991–97). The heritage film was accused of functioning as a selective 'theme park of the past' (Craig 2001: 4) perfectly attuned to the ideological principles of a highly divisive political establishment, and to the interests of the heritage industry as a whole. The meanings of heritage promoted by official culture were necessarily contentious. As John Corner and Sylvia Harvey point out,

> working behind every use of 'heritage' ... there is necessarily a sense of an *inheritance* which is rhetorically projected as 'common', whilst at the same time it is implicitly or contextually closed down around particular characteristics of, for instance, social class, gender and ethnicity. (1991: 49; emphasis in original)

The retrieval of an upper-middle-class and predominantly white English past was a manifestation of the rise of a nationalistic 'folklore from above' (Dave 1997: 117). Other alternative and oppositional heritages, such as the working-class and Black-British experiences, struggled to surface in documentary and experimental work carried out at the margins of the film industry.

In the context of British public culture, the voice of the leftist anti-heritage critics rose with undoubted urgency. The term 'heritage cinema' soon became a byword not so much for a style of filmmaking, but for the ideological mode in which a cycle of films and television serials were deemed to be functioning.[4] In an overview of the debates, Claire Monk has rightly noted that heritage film criticism 'needs to be understood as a historically specific discourse, rooted and responsive to particular cultural conditions and events', which emerged as a negative critique of a cycle of films 'conceived as a "genre" *centrally* engaged in the construction of *national* identity' (2002: 179; emphasis in original). The public endorsement of these tasteful cinematic visions of middle-class culture by voices from the Right further contributed to the creation of an artificial divide that would take root in the critical discourses on British cinema around 1990.[5] Monk (2002) has argued that the wholesale dismissal of what is effectively a popular form of British cinema neglects the actual responses of different kinds of audiences, locking the costume film in an ideological critique akin to the rigid models of 1970s film theory.

The politicisation of the heritage film debates cannot, however, be dissociated from other cultural factors. The mutual influence of the film and tourist industries has furthered a specifically British critique that is deeply suspicious of the visual and narrative pleasures found in the artefacts and practices of the heritage industry. The packaging of the past as an 'experience' in museums and heritage sites transferred well into a strand of film criticism that saw the success of the 1980s British period dramas as part of a larger cultural phenomenon: the commerce of heritage. The high-profile success of the new period dramas for cinema and television tied up with other popular expressions of heritage culture, such as visits to museums and galleries. Consumer spending on heritage centres and trails, including guided visits to properties supported by state bodies such as the National Trust and English Heritage, followed on from the growth in the services sector; as John Hill has noted, 'heritage, in this respect, emerged as an important economic activity and a significant part of the new "enterprise" culture' (1999: 73). It soon became apparent that the consumption of period fictions could operate almost as an extension of guided visits and heritage trails as they involved recreations that transformed the national past into easily comprehensible narratives and spectacular views of objects, landscapes and works of civil architecture. These forms of retro-tourism reinforce the links between the past as an object belonging to visual consumer culture, and popular film and television fictions that derive their prestige from the same literary and historical connections (see Corner & Harvey 1991).

Raphael Samuel has drawn attention to the deep mistrust towards the visual that runs in the anti-heritage critique. Instead, he highlights the democratic potential of heritage culture to interrogate the past. For Samuel, heritage critics deeply object to the transformation (and allegedly, the simplification) of national history into retro styles and tourist kitsch whereby 'heritage is a fraud because it relies on surface appearance' (1994: 262), replacing 'real history' with a history of objects where no active intellectual engagement is necessary – only a distracted 'tourist gaze' (see Urry 1990). Guided tours through heritage properties, coffee-table books and a 'feminine' culture of gifts and souvenirs drawing on Victoriana and Edwardiana (of the kind exploited by commercial franchises such as Past Times or Crabtree and Evelyn) are the most obvious ways in which British history is packaged for tourist consumption. The new heritage film fed the general public's appetite for heritage objects, trading on a nostalgic view of history as an attractive commodity and promising escape into worlds safely located in the past. Massive hits such as the television series *Pride and Prejudice* (BBC, 1995) contributed to the sustained investment in properties managed by National Trust schemes through location fees. Belton House and Sudbury Hall, which were used as the principal locations for the series saw numbers of visitors (domestic and international) rise over 40 per cent (see Sargeant 2000). Likewise, museum and heritage centres increasingly deploy audiovisual materials to support their didactic content, and look to incorporate cinematic elements as part of the visiting experience. This alliance between preservation and reconstruction is arguably a modern equivalent of early connections between film and tourism that go back to the origins of film history (for example, the travelogue genre). The touristic dimension of the heritage genre is not something new, but rather a further stage in the time-travel experiences that film can offer as yet another form of leisure and cultural consumption.

The heritage industry is by no means an exclusively British phenomenon, or one specifically tied to the heritage film genre. It is but one of various aspects of postmodern culture, pertaining to the revival and recycling of past aesthetics in contemporary fashion and the construction of a 'hyper-history', 'inviting us to look at artefacts, buildings and historical reconstructions rather than necessarily understand them in a historical context' (Ludmilla Jordanova quoted in Hill 1999: 76). The anti-heritage critique makes film style instrumental to a specific commercial rationale (the heritage industry). This led Higson to connect the alleged stagnation of film form with the loss of critical representations of history:

> The heritage impulse … is not confined to Thatcherite Britain, but is a characteristic feature of postmodern culture … In this version of history, a critical perspective is displaced by decoration and display … a fascination with style displaces the material dimensions of historical context. The past is reproduced as flat, depthless pastiche, where the reference point is not the past itself, but other images, other texts … The heritage films, too, work as pastiches, each period of the national past reduced through a process of reiteration to an effortlessly reproducible, and attractively consumable, connotative style. (2006: 95)

Higson's critique transfers broader preoccupations around the postmodern into the context of British national cinema. In his analysis, the mixture of popular historicism and the bourgeois appeal of the early films in the trend is symptomatic of the transformation of images of nation into commodities for the international image market, a cultural dominant in what Fredric Jameson has called the era of late or transnational capitalism. Jameson identifies what he deems to be the paradoxical loss of the historical brought about by the new forms of memorialisation; these include a mass-produced culture that endlessly recycles the past in American and European nostalgia films. The heritage film can be considered an example of this phenomenon. Jameson notes that in the nostalgia or 'retro' film, intertextuality emerges as a 'deliberate, built-in feature of the aesthetic effect and as the operator of a new connotation of "pastness" and pseudohistorical depth, in which the history of aesthetic styles displaces "real" history' (1991: 20). These postmodern representations raise anxieties about the ways in which a new visual culture of pastiche and simulacra dominates our relationship with the past, displacing traditional forms of written culture, in particular literary culture.

The heritage film may be just one indicator of the end of political modernisms – its pastiche of the past nothing but a disturbing symptom of our inability to think historically about the present (see Jameson 1991). In this vein, Cairns Craig has argued that the connection between the literary source and its film adaptation in the cycle of films based on Forster's novels (*A Passage to India, A Room with a View, Maurice* and *Where Angels Fear to*

Tread) is 'fundamentally flawed in the relationship they set up between the historical and the contemporary. The audience is invited to understand the plot of the film as though we are *contemporary* with the characters, while at the same time indulging our pleasure in a world which is visually compelling precisely because of its *pastness*' (2001: 4; emphasis in original). However, other critics suggest more dynamic ways of reading the mise-en-scène of the heritage film. The past returns, in the film image as in other manifestations of contemporary culture, through reconstruction rather than preservation, mediated by generic motifs and intertextual references. As Pam Cook puts it, the period film's fascination with the reconstruction of an ultimately imaginary reality reinforces the idea that 'the past in such fictions is never simply the past: they look backwards and forwards at the same time, creating a heterogeneous world that we enter and leave like travellers, in a constant movement of exile and return' (1996: 73). This amounts to a 'present-in-the-past' where the terms 'present' and 'past' are continuously shifting, since contemporary identities evolve in connection with a changing sense of historicity.

New production trends in the British period film since the 1990s have made apparent the limited reach of the ideological critique that simply sees the heritage film as one of the by-products of the political economy of Thatcherism. However, this kind of socio-cultural analysis continues to inform further critical work on the continuities and changes in the heritage films produced during the New Labour period in British politics. The international impact of *Elizabeth* (Shekhar Kapur, 1998), in particular, was also interpreted in the light of its political context. For Pamela Church Gibson, *Elizabeth* marks 'the end of English heritage' (2002: 121), the dismantling of the conventions of authenticity and restraint upheld by the bourgeois heritage film. However, other critics see the film as a symptom of the successful rebranding of a heritage sub-genre – the monarchy film – in the context of the negotiation between tradition and modernity that characterised Tony Blair's terms as Britain's Prime Minister. As Moya Luckett points out,

> During the 90s, Britain has had the challenge of re-imagining itself as ultra-modern while simultaneously being renowned for its history, replacing and re-configuring Thatcherism's combination of economic 'modernity' and veneration of 'heritage' ... [*Elizabeth*]

may be seen in the context of Tony Blair's attempts to update the monarchy by demonstrating how the *image* of a monarch might produce national renown even in the face of very real domestic problems and their potential threat to nationhood. (2000: 90–1; emphasis in original)

Elizabeth modernises the heritage film by infusing it with a baroque mixture of styles, frantic pace and the flashy aesthetics of a conspiracy thriller. Kapur's film rejuvenated the monarchy as a quintessential British icon and re-packaged it for global consumption (see Wayne 2001/2 and 2002). *Elizabeth* re-asserted a myth of national greatness, especially powerful in the face of the challenges to national identity posed by globalisation, Europeanisation and internal devolution.[6] In this respect, the film benefitted from the momentum generated by the short-lived media slogan 'Cool Britannia' that reflected the zeitgeist of economic and artistic confidence at the beginning of Blair's years in office (see Luckett 2000). The ideological implications of the debate surpass the specificity of historical drama; Hill (1999) and Monk (2002) extend the features of the heritage film, such as stereotypical English iconography and upper-class characters, to the national fantasies and touristy London-centric visions of England in evidence in the romantic comedies *Four Weddings and a Funeral* (Mike Newell, 1994), *Notting Hill* (Roger Michell, 1999) and *Bridget Jones's Diary* (Sharon Maguire, 2001), among other films.

Higson's timely yet polemical critique has become an unavoidable point of reference in studies of contemporary British cinema. His initial intervention captured the anti-heritage mood expressed by a broad sector of the Left and defined the heritage film as an almost *de facto* conservative genre, a move that was met with resistance by feminist critics (see Monk 1995, 2001; Cook 1996) for reasons that I will examine in chapter 3. His original argument has continued to evolve leaving substantial room for ambiguity. In subsequent iterations of his own analysis of *Howards End* (1996, 2000, 2003), Higson opens up the *mise-en-scène* of the bourgeois heritage film to a multiplicity of interpretations. He claims that the film directs the distanced gaze of admiring spectatorship towards the display of heritage properties, but also that it gives expression to the conflict between emotional repression and feeling, an aspect that aligns Merchant Ivory's heritage films with the politics of melodrama. Rather than situating the 'truth' of meaning in the text itself, Higson argues that critical interpretations of *Howards End* may change according to journalistic, industrial and reception discourses. Box-office performance, merchandise tie-ins and links with the tourist and heritage industries, let alone the reviewer's own ideological agenda, suggest competing readings. For Higson, the film's emphasis on social relations and class transgression cannot be read in isolation from its ties with the commerce of heritage.

This stance may seem objectionable insofar as it puts on hold a definitive interpretation of the film text (see Harper 2004). However, it also accounts for the continuing critical currency of the heritage film outside and beyond the specific context of Thatcherism, as well as the problematic status of *quality* British cinema and television, to which we shall now turn.

Traditions of quality: negotiating the middlebrow

The heritage film designates cinema's accrued value in terms of its connection to tradition. In an early use of the term 'heritage films', Charles Barr (1986) singles out a cycle of literary and historical dramas that enjoyed popular and critical success during World War II and in the immediate postwar years. This cycle, which includes *That Hamilton Woman/Lady Hamilton* (Alexander Korda, 1941), *The Young Mr Pitt* (Carol Reed, 1942) and *Henry V* (Laurence Olivier, 1944), constituted a visual celebration of Britain's cultural heritage that could be geared towards national propaganda. Two parallel trends informed the profile of British fiction cinema during this period. On the one hand, there were the realist wartime dramas that portrayed the daily lives and sacrifices of ordinary British citizens coping with the stresses of the war effort, such as *Millions Like Us* (Frank Launder and Sidney Gilliat, 1943). On the other was a rich seam of British heritage that could, in times of struggle, be mobilised as an expression of national identity. For example, *Henry V* transformed Shakespeare, one of the pillars of the British literary heritage, into a timely instrument of propaganda. The heritage film in classical British cinema thereby finds itself at the centre of formulations of the national, and appreciated abroad as an expression of the best of British tradition (see Barr 1986; Higson 1995).

As Barr points out, this national narrative wilfully excludes other returns to the past, and other forms of period drama, such as the cycle of escapist historical romps produced by the Gainsborough Studios, 'Ealing's less respectable sister' (1986: 14). The Gainsborough costume dramas presented a point of contention for critics notwithstanding their popularity with domestic audiences, which surpassed that of the realist films (see Cook 1996). Costume hits *The Man in Grey* (Leslie Arliss, 1943), *Madonna of the Seven Moons* (Arthur Crabtree, 1944), *The Wicked Lady* (Leslie Arliss, 1945) and *Jassy* (Bernard Knowles, 1947) were among the most popular films produced by the Gainsborough Studios between 1943 and 1950. Employing exotic locations, glamorous costumes, handsome heroes and adventurous heroines, all of which became a signature of the Gainsborough brand, these costume melodramas targeted female audiences and showed another side to British cinema. Stressing fantasy and excess, the Gainsborough films constitute a marginalised and often despised tradition that was at odds with the preference for realism established by early critical discourses on British cinema. According to Julian Petley these formative discourses demonstrate a 'hostility towards stylisation, the hegemony of the "documentary spirit", the elevation of "contents" over "forms", isolation from wider European artistic trends (and especially from modernism in its various forms) from the 1920s onwards, [and] the conflation of moral prescriptions over aesthetic criteria' (1986: 99–100). These dominant traits crystallised in the views emerging from what Petley calls, after Christian Metz, 'the writing machine': the critical establishment represented by the journalistic work of respected critics Dilys Powell, C. A. Lejeune and Graham Greene. The writing machine helped the formation of British cinema as a national institution by fuelling a normative idea of what British cinema should be like: 'the quality film'.

The terms of this discourse have been outlined by John Ellis (1978, 1996) in his studies of a cross-section of film reviews published in the British press between 1942 and 1948. Ellis notes that film reviewers advocated the notion of the quality film based on humanistic ideals of unity, flow, restraint and contact with 'the real' ('authenticity') as the main elements of value. For these reviewers, realism merged with a moral imperative of truthfulness. Based on an unquestioned belief in the possibility of objectivity in art, 'the real' and 'truth' become interchangeable terms in their writing. In this respect, the 1940s critics defined prescriptive middle-class conceptions of cinema for decades to come (Ellis 1996: 67). Breaching the parameters of authenticity and universality, 'those Gainsborough horrors', as they were described in one of the reviews examined by Ellis (1978: 41), operated as the escapist reverse of the 'consensus film'. The latter's self-effacing realism or appeal to the traditional values and forms of Britain's literary heritage better served cohesive discourses of national identity. Contemporary British settings, issues of national relevance and low-key, tasteful treatments of important subjects were deemed to be the preserve of a realist strand in British cinema, against which the escapist Gainsborough period dramas were judged to be 'foreign' in theme and taste.

These early debates anticipate the problematic place of the heritage film in relation to realism and quality, twin pillars in the formation of discourses of British national cinema. However, the idea of quality cinema that emerged from the critical establishment did not necessarily coincide with the industry's pursuit of overseas box-office success with the 'prestige film' that is, the kind of British film that could break into the American market in particular (see Ellis 1996: 67). This distinction is at the basis of competing discourses about the heritage film. The critical and box-office success of *The Private Life of Henry VIII* (Alexander Korda, 1933) in the United States demonstrated the potential commercial viability of British historical films abroad. Korda's film brought together high production values, an emphasis on visual authenticity in the choice of sets and costumes (including the building of a large set replicating the Great Hall at Hampton Court), and a populist approach to history that stressed a 'private' take on the lives of historical figures. The film achieved an appealing mixture of history and drama that was designed to downplay the intricacies of the historical period, and to emphasise the parallels between past and present (see Harper 1994: 22). Featuring an outstanding performance by Charles Laughton, who plays the monarch as a gluttonous individual driven by his appetites for sex and food, the film combines broad and occasionally bawdy comedy with a pictorial approach that favours a familiar iconography. Held for a few seconds by a stationary camera, the shot that introduces Laughton as Henry VIII famously blocks the actor under an archway in a frontal tableau strongly reminiscent of one of the most famous portraits of the king, painted by Holbein the Younger.[7] From *The Private Life of Henry VIII* to *The Queen*, pictorial references have become a staple feature of the popular monarchy film, alluding to an official history and inserting heritage fictions into a familiar visual tradition.

Throughout the decades, *The Private Life of Henry VIII*, *Tom Jones* (Tony Richardson, 1963), *A Room with a View* and many others have proved the profitability of the British period film, making inroads for British cinema into the international markets in changing industrial and political contexts.[8] However, the idea of quality cinema lost credit as art cinema shifted the focus of criticism in the 1950s from craft and realism to the uniqueness of vision of the individual artist (see Ellis 1996). As the humanist basis of art appreciation entered into crisis after World War II, the belief in film as a work of craftsmanship able to reproduce the exact conditions of existence, or to objectively portray social relations came to be seen as a middle-class construct. In the 1960s, quality cinema started to be displaced by the politicised aesthetic of art cinema and the avant-garde, and the changing tastes of younger and more diverse audiences. As Hill has suggested, the versions of nation on display in the critically valued quality films privileged 'Englishness', or more specifically a distinctive Southern take on white, middle-class Englishness, at the expense of other national (Scottish, Welsh and Irish) and regional identities within the UK; these films were explicitly consensus-seeking as they highlighted the 'elements of "national character" that were regarded as binding the community together' (2001: 33). From the 1960s Free Cinema to Black British cinemas in the 1970s and the 'state of the nation' films of the 1980s, realism has progressively lost its consensual connotations, taking on instead the politically charged agenda of oppositional cinema. Throughout the 1960s and 1970s the period film remained a resilient popular genre that occasionally intersected strands of modernism and critical realism in British cinema, as in Joseph Losey's *The Go-Between* (1970) or Stanley Kubrick's *Barry Lyndon* (1975). The debates about the 1980s heritage films brought the backlash against middle-class 'quality' and 'restraint' to the fore, branding them as ideologically biased concepts (see Monk 2002: 184). However, it is the central yet problematic position that the quality film occupies in the mapping of contemporary British cinema that makes its aesthetic and economic implications more apparent.

In the 1980s the notion of quality became the basis of the exportability of British cinema and television programmes, while it was also reinforced by the aesthetic, institutional and economic convergence between both mediums (see Caughie 2000). The success of *Chariots of Fire* and *A Room with a View* spearheaded a short-lived 'renaissance' in British cinema. *A*

Room with a View achieved wide exposure in the American market, by way of a shrewd campaign of slow roll-out release that benefited from positive critical reception and word of mouth. The film, a modest $3 million production, went on to gross $25 million in the US and more than $68 million worldwide (see Higson 2003). This success cannot be dissociated from the popularity of two Granada productions, the Raj-set serial *The Jewel in the Crown* (1984) and *Brideshead Revisited*, aired by the commercial British television channel ITV (Independent Television) in 1981 and by PBS (Public Broadcasting Service) in the US in 1982. Adapted from the eponymous novel by Evelyn Waugh and partially set in Oxford, *Brideshead Revisited* looks at the rarefied milieu of an aristocratic Catholic family during the interwar period. More than any other television serial up to this point, it helped to consolidate the notion of British quality programming by virtue of its connections with highbrow traditions. In a critique that bears strong parallels to the heritage film debate in the work by Wollen, Higson and Craig, Charlotte Brunsdon notes the following about *The Jewel in the Crown* and *Brideshead Revisited*:

> Formally unchallenging, while nevertheless replete with visual strategies that signify 'art', their only specifically televisual demand is that the viewer switch on at the right time and watch. Just like the National Trust and advertisements for wholemeal bread, they produce a certain image of England and Englishness which is untroubled by contemporary division and guaranteed aesthetic legitimacy. (1990: 86)

According to Brunsdon the four markers of quality present in these productions, that is, a 'literary source', 'the best of British acting', 'money' (in lieu of an expensive look) and 'heritage export' appeal, are also visible in some of the most successful British heritage films of the 1980s (ibid.). The repetition of these components indicates an emerging pattern towards the internationalisation and commercialisation of a successful format (see Krewani 2004). The continuing success of British heritage films and classic serials in the 1990s, most notably the adaptations of Jane Austen novels for film and television, including *Sense and Sensibility* (Ang Lee, 1995) and the six-part BBC series *Pride and Prejudice* scripted by Andrew Davies, has contributed to the cementing of an image of modern British quality cinema and television as a showcase for strong literary and acting traditions.

This strong profile rests on the appeal of the middlebrow. As Lawrence Napper (2000; 2009) notes, the idea of the middlebrow began to come to the fore in mainstream British culture during the interwar years, at the same time as the country experienced a rapid growth in mass communication media. As a new category that resulted from the gradual fusion of the highbrow and the lowbrow, the middlebrow encapsulated anxieties over cultural distinctions motivated by the social and cultural dynamism that characterised British society at the time. The rise of a middlebrow British cinema in the 1920s and 1930s was supported by the suburban middle classes as distinct from the consumption of Hollywood cinema. This fading of cultural barriers, symptomatic of the cultural aspirations of a newly formed middle class, was regarded with suspicion by the intellectual establishment. Napper, however, associates the middlebrow with class mobility and the fruitful blurring of boundaries between media occurring during this period. He notes that the middlebrow was infused with optimism regarding the creation (not exempt of tensions) of a common national culture through mass media forms, a project that would crystallise in the cinema of consensus of the World War II years.

Some of these connotations live on in the British film culture of the final decades of the twentieth century, where they were problematically reasserted as negative markers of persistent class and economic divisions against the grain of a fully democratised commercial culture. The popularity of Merchant Ivory's English-themed films prompted US-based scholar Martin A. Hipsky to coin the expression 'Anglophil(m)ia' (1994). For Hipsky, the quality film becomes an expression of cultural capital, rendering the opposition between highbrow art and mass entertainment increasingly irrelevant. In an argument reminiscent of Higson's dichotomy between narrative and heritage space (2006), Hipsky describes the generic images of high culture deployed by the 1980s films (such as Oxford and Cambridge, the English country house or the art of the Italian Renaissance) as subordinated to an idea of social realism superfluous in terms of plot and character portrayal. For Hipsky, such allusions bring 'an *excess* of signification that is unironically meant to provide great sensual pleasure' (1994: 102; emphasis in original). The effectiveness of this critique relies, however, not on close analysis of the films' intrinsic cinematic features, but on the sociological function of quality as a specialist niche product. Thus, Hipsky claims, the textual markers of highbrow culture that characterise the Forster literary adaptations made by Merchant Ivory trade on class appeal for educated audiences who 'want their increasingly expensive college education to pay some cultural dividends' and therefore seek a mode of entertainment that gratifies their sense of 'cultural *entitlement*' (1994: 103, emphasis in original).

This critique indirectly links to a shift in the way audiences were targeted. Hollywood studios had begun to set up their own 'independent' production and distribution channels to nurture specialist fare and to capitalise on niche audiences not catered for by the average blockbuster product. For Esther Sonnet, the quality film denotes the 'convergence of the exercise of class-determined extratextual "taste" with the specifically filmic conditions of popular cinema that identify an intrinsic and distinguishing mode of cinema spectatorship' (1999: 56). Sonnet notes that the pleasures offered by the 'literary film' not only include 'spectacular excess' but also the absence of mainstream eroticism in favour of a more subtle expression of sexuality, which invites a mode of 'genteel' spectatorship 'superior' to that demanded by mainstream film narratives. The over-investment in '"the look", in gestures, fleeting glances, failed speech, clamped emotions and frustrated intentions' make for a mode of address that dwells on the pleasurable performance of repression, and presents a distinctive alternative to mainstream commercial genres (1999: 57–8). For example, the heritage attractions of *Howards End* presented a marked alternative to the graphic sexual thrills of *Basic Instinct* (Paul Verhoeven, 1992), which hit North American cinemas in the same month. Although unable to compete on the same scale as the Hollywood blockbuster, *Howards End*'s phased release, positive reviews in the mainstream press and award recognition allowed the film to capitalise on its popularity with older audiences at upmarket cinemas and to make its mark as a crossover success.[9] As already noted, the middlebrow quality film seemingly invites a number of interpretations. Famously derided as an example of the aesthetically indulgent 'Laura Ashley School of filmmaking' (Higson 2003: 181),[10] *Howards End* can also be read as a tasteful piece of Edwardiana, a politically suspect meditation on Englishness and single motherhood (see Stone 2004) or as a progressive drama with an emphasis on class criticism. By aiming for the middle ground, the quality heritage film risks falling between two stools, neither genuine art nor genuinely popular (see Higson 2003). In practice, therefore, the association with the middlebrow tends to establish conservative readings as the dominant readings.

The focus on the middlebrow has contributed to the consolidation of the idea of one ongoing generic cycle, albeit one formulated and sustained through academic discourse rather than reflected in industrial patterns. It has also highlighted critical anxieties about the absence of a strong modernist tradition in British cinema, the popularisation of high culture and the hybrid nature of popular culture including the fluid links between stage, screen and television. Playwrights like Stephen Poliakoff and Alan Bennett and theatre directors like Richard Eyre and Trevor Nunn have used the heritage film as a vehicle for moving across different media within their thematic comfort zones, whilst diverse generations of stage actors including Laurence Olivier, Anthony Hopkins, Emma Thompson, Judi Dench, Daniel Day Lewis, Ralph Fiennes or Ben Wishaw have forged or advanced their star personas with performances that display 'actorliness' (Hill 1999: 82) and the mastery of the literary word. In this respect, the performance of emotional restraint (see Sonnet, above) that recurs in many heritage films builds on historical constructions of Englishness that entertain complex links with the traditions of realism and melodrama (see Dyer 1994).

The middlebrow aspect of the heritage film debate has been interrogated more in terms of what it excludes than of what it actually entails. The debates have tended to neglect films that, in retrospect, do not fit the success story of 1980s heritage cinema, films which propose alternative fictions of the national and films closer to the popular and art cinema. As Sheldon Hall (2009) has noted, the map of the heritage film would look very different had it included from the beginning the overtly populist (the Gainsborough and Hammer outputs); the baroque and the excessive (Ken Russell's *Gothic*, 1986); the avant-garde (Peter Greenaway's *The Draughtsman's Contract*, 1982, or Derek Jarman's *Caravaggio*, 1986); the poetic and the autobiographical (Terence Davies' *Distant Voices, Still Lives*, 1988); or the international co-productions (and American runaway productions) that chronologically precede the formulation of the heritage critique, and which often wear auteurist credentials (*Tom Jones*, *Barry Lyndon* or Roman Polanski's *Tess*, 1979). These works display neither the self-effacing craftsmanship nor the belief in the codes of realism that make for the quality connotations of the heritage style.

In particular, auteurist and heritage discourses remarkably exclude each other. The personalities of filmmakers with a distinct track record outside the genre tend to be subsumed into the generic cycles against which the films are read. For example, independent Canadian director Patricia Rozema's queer inflection of *Mansfield Park* (1999); Mira Nair's distinctive transcultural vision of *Vanity Fair* (2004); and Polanski's new version of *Oliver Twist* (2005) introduce subtle stylistic and thematic variations rather than radical reworkings of period mise-en-scène in the manner of avant-garde outsiders such as Greenaway. Industrially, the above films tick all the boxes of upmarket fare, offering superficially pretty recreations of reputed literary classics suitable to family audiences. However, a closer look at Polanski's version of *Oliver Twist* makes 'auteur' sense if read as a follow-up to *The Pianist* (2002), Polanski's classical narrative-style take on the Holocaust film. The cruel details of everyday life for the street children in London's underbelly in *Oliver Twist* resonate with the ghettoised poverty and anxieties about confinement, resourcefulness and survival in the face of historical trauma that are at work in *The Pianist*. Furthermore, *The Pianist* raises provocative questions about crisis areas of historical filmmaking, and the Holocaust film in particular, becoming 'heritage' as they become an industry (and a genre) in themselves. Perhaps most paradoxically, at the time of writing James Ivory and the late Ismail Merchant, independent filmmakers who more than any others constitute a recognised 'brand', are yet to be the object of a critical reappraisal as fully-fledged auteurs.

The meanings of middlebrow aesthetics present one of the most interesting challenges for the reassessment of the heritage film. As Robert Murphy notes, 'there is a sad irony in the way in which, just as flamboyant melodramas and gothic horror films have achieved a certain respectability, cool, intelligent films like *A Passage to India* … and *A Room with a View* … are pushed out beyond the pale, as if fantasy must necessarily exclude realism and vice versa' (2001: 2). Taking into account the diverse critical investments in the idea of the national, and the charges of cultural commodification and historical revisionism, it is not exaggerated to claim that the middlebrow remains the last frontier of film studies; the denigrated centre of British production isolated by the fetishisation of the 'edges' (see Napper 2000: 110). However, anxieties about the middlebrow are compounded by another set of arguments that look at the heritage film as a *bona fide* popular British genre.

Heritage and convergence: television and the idea of British cinema

Television has paved the way for the continuing success of heritage films in the 1990s and the 2000s. UK broadcasters BBC and Channel Four have forged partnerships with top independent film companies such as Working Title, Miramax and the Weinstein Company, as well as the Hollywood studios. These alliances function as a two-way flow of personnel, funds and concepts that benefit from the distinctive possibilities offered by each medium. The British film industry, described by James Leggott as a 'fragmentary cottage industry of small, undercapitalised independent companies, which now and again enjoy a one-off commercial breakthrough' (2008: 15), is notorious for its instability. Largely deprived of state support, the interdependence between film and television has helped to define the British film production sector in crucial ways. In the 1980s Channel Four Films, the film production arm of the broadcaster Channel Four, sustained independent filmmakers working in formats indebted to television drama with auteurist ambitions.[11] The BBC would follow a decade later with its own film production outfit, BBC Films, notable for its investment in period films, often in partnership with North American production companies.

John Caughie (2000) has pointed out the gradual evolution from the prestigious British art cinema of the 1980s towards the more predictable and marketable signs of quality and high production values that characterised the 1990s. This development parallels the progressive move of resources away from the television play and into the serial instead, a more sustainable format that is also more marketable in an economy increasingly dependent on overseas sales. The heritage aesthetic has given the literary adaptation a central role in the image of British cinema abroad, but it is quality television, and in particular the classical serial, that has cemented the relationship between the two. As Sarah Cardwell points out, *Brideshead Revisited* in the 1980s and *Pride and Prejudice* in the 1990s established the 'classic-novel adaptation' as a genre central to the canon of television drama, with their salient features of fidelity, nostalgia and quality (2002: 129). For Cardwell, textual markers, such as patterns of framing and editing, highlight the heritage aesthetic of *Brideshead Revisited*. The long shots over Castle Howard (the Yorkshire estate that doubled as the titular seat of the Marchmain family), the use of wide-angle lenses, deep focus and high-key lighting schemes stress the grandeur of each extensive set. These aspects also accentuate a 'directed, structured and particular' sense of stasis and nostalgia that is internal to the text (2002: 123). The extended use of Charles Ryder's (Jeremy Irons) omniscient narration through flashbacks and voice-overs highlights the serial's obsessive fidelity to the source novel; yet the uniqueness of this relationship is mediated by a series of traits that reappear in subsequent films and television serials. For example, countryside travelling sequences shot from carriages or horseback (modes of transport that accentuate the 'pastness' of the landscape) and interior scenes orchestrated around ritualised acts such as afternoon tea or the social ball, became typical set-pieces that could be re-adapted and extended to other period serials, and even contemporary dramas like the Oxford-set *Inspector Morse* (ITV, 1987–2000). Cardwell notes that these features became signifiers of quality television drama; these serials do not necessarily seek to imitate the cinematic experience, but they signal continuity with films such as *Chariots of Fire* and *Maurice*. This uniformity of style and tone is also noticeable in Julian Jarrold's film version of *Brideshead Revisited* (2008), a film that can be viewed as an adaptation of the television mini-series, rather than as an adaptation of the literary original.

The classic serial's quality markers (a literary source, the best of British acting, an expensive look and exportability as a heritage product) were arguably set in the 'stone' of a fully-fledged genre by the overwhelming success of the BBC series *Pride and Prejudice*. In this 1995 classic Jane Austen adaptation, nostalgia becomes a mood that is generic and diffuse rather than specific to its particular narrative. In the opening episode, point-of-view shots inscribe character motivation onto the spectacular mise-en-scène of the heritage landscape, creating an immediate bond of identification with the protagonist Elizabeth Bennet (Jennifer Ehle). At the same time, the series banishes a constraining servitude to the novel and relies instead on established generic tropes that function as 'shortcuts' to desired affects (see Cardwell 2002: 149). The script by Davies notoriously added narrative twists, such as Darcy's swim in the lake and subsequent encounter with Elizabeth, which became a celebrated moment in the series. In Cardwell's words *Pride and Prejudice* developed into a 'contemporary and popular event, and not a restrained retelling of a worthy literary classic' (2002: 156). In this instance the serial's organic relationship with the source text is taken over by a new mode of historicity that arises from the status of the televisual as a popular, participatory and performative event, linked to the extratextual ways in which *Pride and Prejudice* defined a singular moment in British television of the 1990s. The high audience ratings of the series impacted on magazine covers and ancillary products (most notably the VHS and, later, the DVD package). Rather than maintaining the 'assumption of cultural hegemony associated to the "quality" literary adaptation' (De Groot 2009: 190), *Pride and Prejudice* brought to the fore the adaptation as a televisual event that expresses nation and community 'from below'.

Pride and Prejudice was a stepping stone in the Jane Austen boom of the 1990s, yet one that crucially contributed to diminish the role of the original literary text and to enhance the sense of a generic cycle. Lee's *Sense and Sensibility*, from 1995; the feature-film *Emma* (Douglas McGrath, 1996); the ITV version of *Emma* (1996), scripted by Davies; *Persuasion* (1995), directed by Roger Michell for television but given a theatrical release in the US; Rozema's Miramax-produced *Mansfield Park*; the new Austen trilogy (including new versions of *Mansfield Park*, *Northanger Abbey* and *Persuasion*) that was aired back to back on ITV in March and April 2007, and on PBS' 'Masterpiece' slot in early 2008; and the new BBC productions of *Sense and Sensibility* in 2008 and *Emma* in 2009 show, with minimal but intriguing variations, the continuing success of the 'Austen on screen' formula. Davies' three-part 2008 adaptation of *Sense and Sensibility* for the BBC opens with an erotic sequence that prefigures the main narrative. This kind of addition, whilst executed within the tasteful expectations set by the mise-en-scène of the quality adaptation, speaks volumes about the genrification of the Austen franchise and the 'update' of the markers of quality to attract new audiences. The full transformation of Austen's novels into icons of popular culture continues with the 'Austen without Austen' trend of the 2000s. *Bride and Prejudice* (Gurindher Chadha, 2004); *Becoming Jane* (Julian Jarrold, 2007); *The Jane Austen Book Club* (Robin Swicord, 2007) as well as the television biopic *Miss Austen Regrets* (BBC, 2008) and the fantasy mini-series *Lost in Austen* (ITV, 2008) (in which a twenty-first-century London girl finds a magic door that transports her into the world of *Pride and Prejudice*) confirm the generic status of the Austen phenomenon whilst dispensing with the incorporation of the literary text.

The role of television as a creative and economic motor behind new cycles of heritage films should not be understimated. In 1998, Chanel Four Films became Film Four, a production arm with mini-studio ambitions that raised the stakes in film production. The heritage film appeared to be a safe means of repositioning British filmmaking in the global market (see Hill 2001; Macnab 2002; Roddick 2007). Channel Four's involvement in the development of British heritage films had paid off with the international success of *The Madness of King George* (Nicholas Hytner, 1994) and *Elizabeth*. The latter shook off the quaint veneer of the quality heritage film, bringing the genre closer to the grand scale and commercial ambitions of Hollywood historical drama. The dangers of this strategy became clear when World War II drama *Charlotte Gray* (Gillian Armstrong, 2001), also starring Cate Blanchett, failed to deliver. The film, which was budgeted at £12 million, made a meagre £1.3 million at the UK box office, a loss that precipitated the demise of the Film Four production venture. By contrast, BBC Films has successfully 'carved a niche for both heritage cinema on the small scale ... and "quality" (i.e. small screen) drama writ slightly larger than on TV' (Roberts & Wallis 2007: 22). In this respect, little separates the mise-en-scène of BBC Films' biopics *Iris* (Richard Eyre, 2001) and *Sylvia* (Christine Jeffs, 2003) from the quality drama produced directly for television, such as the Philip Larkin biopic *Love Again* (BBC, 2003). Convergence at the level of production continues to inform the functional, self-effacing style of British literary adaptations (see Leggott 2008: 51), such as *The History Boys* (Nicholas Hytner, 2006), *Notes on a Scandal* (Richard Eyre, 2006) and *The Reader* (Stephen Daldry, 2008), whereas the 'hybrid' or 'televisual' aesthetics of the historical genre, which promotes the economic synergy between film and television, is a feature not only of British television but also in other European countries like France (see Ostrowska 2007: 145).

Increasingly, the markers of quality do not necessarily place 'Britishness' (or, more precisely, 'Englishness') in the past, but rather reposition strong theatrical and literary traditions in contemporary television. Over the years, the relationship between quality television and the heritage film has become not only economically beneficial, but also mutually enriching from an aesthetic viewpoint. For example, the gothic narratives of feminine entrapment at the centre of *The Tenant of Wildfell Hall* (BBC, 1996) and *Daniel Deronda* (BBC, 2002) historicise gender violence in ways that are reminiscent of the feminist films of Jane Campion, *The Piano* and *The Portrait of a Lady* (1996) (see Caughie 2000: 218). The paranoid aesthetic (jarring editing, obtrusive camera angles and masked shots) of the television series *Bleak House* (BBC, 2005) transferred well to the big-screen adaptation *The Other Boleyn Girl* (2008), both directed by Justin Chadwick. The historical novel by Philippa Gregory that serves as basis for this film had previously been adapted for television under the same title (*The Other Boleyn Girl*, BBC 2003). This production borrowed dramatic devices characteristic of reality television shows such as *Big Brother* (Channel Four, 2000–10), for example having the main female characters intermittently address the camera from a closed space that evokes the diary room featured in the Channel Four programme. Sarah Street points out that the feminist aspirations of this BBC adaptation met with critical charges of sensationalism, with some critics dismissing the show as '"low-brow" nonsense' (2004: 105). Nevertheless, as Street notes, *The Other Boleyn Girl* qualifies alongside highbrow quality dramas (for example, Stephen Poliakoff's *The Lost Prince*, BBC, 2003) and historical docudramas as self-reflexive instances of postmodern heritage television. Likewise, the fusion of the soap-opera format with the classical serial in *Bleak House* and *Little Dorrit* (BBC, 2008) creates a new 'syncretic' heritage product that seeks to attract a wider integrated (soap/costume/heritage) audience (see Voigts-Virchow 2004: 24).

The interface between the heritage film and quality television in the 2000s (not to mention the proliferation of formats and cycles) manifests in a wide range of styles that are not amenable to a unique ideological reading. Yet the question remains whether the success of the heritage genre has actually opened a space for political content. The revisionist Victorian narratives *Tipping the Velvet* (BBC, 2002) and *Fingersmith* (BBC, 2005), adapted from hit novels by Sarah Waters, went a long way in queering quality television, putting sexual politics and lesbian identities firmly on the agenda of a genre with a dominant heteronormative history. British television's strong tradition of radical political drama also informs English Civil War drama *The Devil's Whore* (Channel Four, 2008). Written by Peter Flannery, who also penned *Our Friends in the North* (BBC, 1996), its edgy visuals mix a pastiche of Baroque styles, evoked through dark colours and contrasted, expressionistic lighting.

Off-centre framing and fast-paced cutting bring immediacy to the series' focus on the sexual and political mobility of Angelica Fanshawe (Andrea Riseborough). Whilst Angelica is a throwback to the pleasure-seeking heroines of the Gainsborough melodramas, she is also endowed with a social identity that matures through the ravaged landscapes of a

An unconventional heroine: Angelica Fanshawe joins the egalitarian cause in *The Devil's Whore*

national history driven forward by instability and violent internal clashes that allow little room for durable romance. Although this spectacular vision of the Civil War period is a far cry from the modernist radicalism of Peter Watkins' *Culloden* (BBC, 1964) or Bill Douglas' *Comrades* (1986), *The Devil's Whore*'s focus on class struggle and the corruption of egalitarian causes expands the possibilities of popular heritage television for direct political commentary.

Quality television constantly renews its appeal and expands its market by adapting the 'classic serial' label, sometimes beyond recognition, to the tastes of new generations of spectators. Key to this transformation are performers with crossover appeal. The genre has defined the star personas of Colin Firth and Keira Knightley, and keeps providing a platform for young British actors, such as Romola Garai, Carey Mulligan and James McAvoy. Just as important is the distinctive work of 'star' tele-vision writers such as Andrew Davies, Michael Hirst and Peter Morgan, which has introduced distinctive auteurist styles into established generic frameworks.[12] With his scripts for *Pride and Prejudice, The Fortunes and Misfortunes of Moll Flanders* (ITV, 1996), *Vanity Fair* (BBC, 1998) and *Tipping the Velvet* Davies has established a strong reputation for sexing up the classical serial while upholding the theme of emotional repression that runs through his nineteenth-century material. Hirst's scripts for *Elizabeth: The Golden Age* (Shekhar Kapur, 2007), the delayed sequel to *Elizabeth*, and the transatlantic series *The Tudors* (BBC, 2007–10), update the Elizabethan monarchy drama with abundant doses of sex and violence. The latter series profitably merges British costume drama tradition with the high production values and global reach of North American television. Finally, Morgan's work offers perhaps the most consistent and effortless example of the crossover between political drama and the heritage genre, in films like *The Last King of Scotland* (Kevin Macdonald, 2006), *The Other Boleyn Girl* and *The Queen*.

The multiple facets of British heritage television since the 2000s undo any monolithic definition of 'quality'. Instead, the structures of collaboration and convergence built throughout the 1980s and 1990s have created a solid model of production and distribution that aims to cater to the tastes of national audiences and to compete in the crowded international market for the label of 'good television'. As Cardwell (2007) notes, the old markers of quality have now migrated to a different kind of programme associated with the innovation and high production values of contemporary American drama. The markers of 'quality television' established in the early 1990s have been outgrown by new values and a greater diversity of content shaped by the demands of the globalised market. On this basis, we may prefer to examine the new cycles of heritage television as simply 'good television' instead of 'quality television'.

This section has drawn on a variety of examples in order to highlight television's contribution to the formation of Britain's heritage film culture. This phenomenon needs to be taken into account when considering the map of forces shaping British national cinema, and the prominent role that the heritage film plays within it. In the final section of this chapter, the arguments developed so far are drawn upon to support an analysis of *The Queen* in order to examine further the evolving discourses of nation and the hybrid aesthetics of the monarchy film.

The Queen and the monarchy film

Can a film set in 1997 be considered a heritage film? This is one of the questions that this section will try to answer as it examines the ways in which *The Queen*, released in 2006, brings up to date a tradition of monarchy films that dramatise the private lives of their royal protagonists. In particular, the dialogue between cinematic and televisual elements brings to the fore discourses about nation and representation that are central to the heritage film debate. The familiar past staged by the film is no less reconstructed than that of the more elaborate historical spectacles in other British monarchy films. Yet the very closeness in time and experience between narrative content and production context invites us to consider the shifting boundary between dynamic renderings of history and static representations of heritage. Here it is proposed that *The Queen* can be viewed as a key heritage film on the grounds of its incisive and often poignant reflection on national identity at a moment in which a post-national British cinema is coming to the fore.

The monarchy film, which places actual royal figures at the centre of fictionalised stories, is a generic sub-cycle that has contributed greatly to establishing the heritage film as the British genre most concerned with tradition and nostalgia for the (imperial) past. The lives of monarchs have inspired spectacular films from *The Private Life of Henry VIII* to *Elizabeth: The Golden Age*. They also lend themselves for exploration of moments of political crisis, as in *The Madness of King George*. *The Queen* brings together both elements. Set during the week following the death of Diana, Princess of Wales, in a car crash in Paris in August 1997, the film focuses on the differing responses of the Queen (Helen Mirren) and the Royal Family, and the then freshly-elected Prime Minister Tony Blair (Michael Sheen) to the unprecedented outpouring of public sentiment that followed. The film's concern with the overlap between the private and the public in an era of mass-mediated events is dramatised via the negotiation between two ideological positions and political agendas: the Queen's inflexible upholding of the traditional values of duty and emotional restraint is contrasted with Blair's strategic management of the media frenzy surrounding Diana's death.

Scripted by Peter Morgan and directed by Stephen Frears, *The Queen* was developed as a television project for Granada and eventually became a European co-production with Italian and French capital. *The Queen* followed Morgan and Frears' successful collaboration in *The Deal* (Channel Four, 2003), a television drama about Tony Blair's rise to the leadership of New Labour over his friend and party colleague Gordon Brown. *The Queen*, in which Sheen reprises the role of Blair after *The Deal*, also focuses on the balance of power and its shifts (see Kemp 2006). This theme has established Morgan's auteur credentials as a playwright and scriptwriter of political dramas based on actual historical figures in period settings, namely *The Last King of Scotland*, *The Other Boleyn Girl* and *Frost/Nixon* (based on Morgan's own stage play and made into a film by Ron Howard in 2008). *The Special Relationship* (BBC, 2010) confirms the success of a dramatic formula that has allowed Morgan to alternate smaller biographical projects focused on events and characters from British cultural history (such as the television docudrama *Longford* (BBC, 2006) and the comedy *The Damned United* (2009), both directed by Tom Hooper) with more high-concept explorations of Anglo-American politics that strategically aim at the US market. The close and productive relationship between film and television that underpins these films, including *The Queen*, reframes moments and events from twentieth-century history as heritage.

Like the other films scripted by Morgan *The Queen* is structured around character confrontation and political negotiation between two individuals with opposing views on power and its handling. The film's emotional focus falls on Elizabeth II's struggle to cope publicly with the high tide of sentiment caused by the death of Princess Diana, and privately with the pressures placed on her as Head of State and (the film suggests) as the head of a dysfunctional family. In this respect, *The Queen* continues a cycle of 1990s heritage films that present the monarchy in crisis, in danger of losing its function as a role model and symbol of a unified nation (see McKechnie 2002). Kara McKechnie notes that the portrayal offered by the royal biopic has been consistent with the perceived function of the monarchy at the moment of production. The royal biopic tends to offer sober portraits in times of crisis, as in *Victoria the Great* (Herbert Wilcox, 1938), which functioned as a reassuring validation of the monarchy after the Abdication Crisis of 1936. Conversely, in times of stability the royal biopic can even indulge in parody, as seen in the American film *Beau Brummell* (Curtis Bernhardt, 1954). For McKechnie, the resurgence of the royal biopic in the 1990s is partly due to the new position of the royals at the centre of a high-profile celebrity culture following the media interest in the successive crises that affected the House of Windsor, especially the breakdown of Charles and Diana's marriage in the mid-1990s and Diana's death in August 1997.

The monarchy biopic of the 1990s became increasingly self-reflective about the narratives of history and nation, fulfilling a myth-making (and myth-breaking) function that is difficult to dissociate from the evolving media narratives around Diana's transformation from fairytale princess in the early 1980s to suffering soap-opera heroine in the 1990s (see Geraghty 1998). The unorthodox portrait of Elizabeth I produced in Kapur's *Elizabeth*, which presented her as a romantic and sexually active young woman at the centre of political intrigue was remarkably attuned to the irresistible rise of Diana as the new face of an old institution in the post-feminist age. Indeed, the impact of her sensational death may have helped to boost the box office success of *Elizabeth* and to inflect the reception of *Mrs Brown* (John Madden, 1997), released in the UK just a few days after the event.[13] In *The Queen* the death of Diana provides the narrative context and also functions as a haunting intertext that underpins the overlap between private and public histories in an age of image saturation.

In its aesthetics of restraint *The Queen* is closer to *Mrs Brown* than it is to *Elizabeth*. *Mrs Brown* focuses on Queen Victoria's long period of mourning following the death of her husband, Prince Albert, and chronicles her relationship with her personal servant John Brown; it presents a monarch both emotionally and physically trapped as much by the regimented hierarchy in the royal residences as by her role. Like *Mrs Brown*, *The Queen* explores the disjunction between a monarch's public and private personas and boasts a central performance by an actor of international reputation as its greatest asset (see Leggott 2008: 79). Mirren brings memories of previous roles to the part: the supportive Queen Charlotte in *The Madness of King George*, a mature queen in the mini-series *Elizabeth I* (Channel Four, 2005) and, especially, the tenacious DCI Jane Tennison in the long-running series *Prime Suspect* (ITV, 1991–2006). Her performance in the latter, in particular, stresses the solitude of a female professional in a tough, hyper-masculine milieu, adding further credibility to her turn as Elizabeth II.

Both Judi Dench as Queen Victoria and Helen Mirren as Queen Elizabeth II dominate their films with extremely controlled performances. Often shot in close-up, both actresses dramatise emotional restraint through small, contained gestures. The focus on facial expression, the modulation of the voice and the precise but self-effacing quality of background period detail enhance the realism of their play. These aspects contribute to nuanced psychological portraits of the otherwise inaccessible figures they embody and single out the 'star-as-performer' as the main attraction of the monarchy film.[14] Unlike the spectacular *Elizabeth*, *Mrs Brown* and *The Queen* are suited to domestic consumption as quality television, as well as working as star-powered heritage films that did well in theatres. In both films historical crises prompt reflection on the competing meanings of the nation, but the primary focus falls on the female monarch's personal struggle to resolve the tension between duty and desire. In a key sequence in *The Queen*, the friction between the Queen and the newly elected Prime Minister escalates after she is repeatedly obliged to listen to Blair's advice on how to address the tide of public sentiment following Diana's death. The Queen's growing impatience is shown through distracted gestures, such as cleaning her glasses and rearranging objects on a desk, whilst she listens to Blair on the speakerphone. She finally grabs the receiver to berate Blair for giving in to pressure from the press. Following a cut from a long to a medium shot, a melancholic, muffled string theme is introduced in the background. The camera subtly tracks in on Mirren's face, as she delivers some of her most emblematic lines in the film:

> It is my belief that they [the British people] will any moment reject this ... this mood, which has been stirred up by the press, in favour of a period of restrained grief and sober, private mourning [cut to close-up of Blair looking sceptical]. That's the way we do things in this country, quietly, with dignity. That's what the rest of the world has always admired us for.

The reference to 'essential' facets of the British national character and the speech's self-conscious staging of conflictive definitions of the nation's imagined community give this scene a pivotal role in the film. Previous films like *Mrs Brown* make the historically distant figure of the monarch relevant to contemporary audiences through the theme of emotion as transgression in an age of restraint. Conversely, *The Queen* sympathetically presents the predicament of the modern ruler as a defence of restraint in an age of emotion. The inflexibility of Elizabeth II in the face of change betrays an institution in crisis in a film that ironically portrays the royal family as an out-of-touch clan holding the fort on an island of privilege, impervious to the urgency of events as represented by the torrent of tele-visual images. Humorous episodes, such as the Queen Mother's shocked reaction at the idea of Diana 'stealing' the plans for her own funeral, are used to demonstrate the extent to which some members of the Royal Family just 'don't get it'. The Queen's failure to grasp the significance of this instance of history-in-the-making, and her ideological appropriation

of the values of dignity and restraint via a language that evokes imperial politics do not fundamentally invalidate perceived traditional British
values or the monarchy's symbolic alignment with them. By contrasting
notions of transience and permanence, the film assesses the legacy of a
historical moment during which one of Britain's ancient institutions was
severely questioned by the rise of a new political class in touch with public
sensibilities. In this respect, the dialogue between cinema and television
produces a commentary on historical processes that are still open.

The textures of heritage: painting, cinema, television

The Queen opens with a quotation from Part II of William Shakespeare's
Henry IV ('uneasy lies the head that wears a crown'), and brief images
from a newscast about New Labour's landslide victory accompanied by the
voice of veteran newsreader Jon Snow. In these first seconds of the film,
the television screen invades the film frame delivering factual information
about the events of 1997, even if the footage is a reconstruction that introduces Sheen and Helen McCrory in the roles of Tony and Cherie Blair.

This opening sequence uses television as the primary source of historical context, while at the same time directing our attention to the different
texture of the electronic image (shot in 16mm) within the cinematic mise-
en-scène. It is quickly revealed that the images are coming from a television set that the Queen is watching while posing for an official portrait.
The sense of history-in-the-making is double as it arises from the grainy
newscast images as well as from the canvas in progress. The painter, Mr
Crawford, is initially only an offscreen voice that responds to the Queen's
question, prompted by the television programme, 'have you voted yet, Mr
Crawford?' A reverse-shot then discloses the identity of the actor playing
Mr Crawford, Bermuda-born Earl Cameron, the leading black actor in British
social-problem films such as *Sapphire* (Basil Dearden, 1959) and *Flame in
the Streets* (Roy Ward Baker, 1961). Cameron's cameo brings to the fore
issues of race, nation and in/exclusiveness, which are ironically deflected
by the conservative views expressed by his character. Mr Crawford claims
not to have voted for Mr Blair (and therefore, in the Queen's words, he is
not a 'moderniser'), because of the danger of losing 'too much that is good
about this country as it is'. This moment of relaxed complicity between
the sovereign and the royal painter, and their rapport in the shared space

of the frame despite the physical and social distance between them enhances the status of Elizabeth II as Queen of all the British people in more tangible ways than the televisual images of Blair and the multiple close-ups of his enthusiastic supporters. Television momentarily intrudes into the spectacle of continuity and tradition, signified by painting and filmed in 35mm (see Burdeau 2006: 33). The opening sequence closes with the soundtrack's main theme as the star's name above the title ('Helen Mirren') appears over a fade-to-black, which cuts to a mobile shot that starts on the Queen's feet and tilts upwards to her face, showing her dressed in full regalia against a neutral gray background. The camera stays on Mirren's face for about six seconds. Then, somewhat mechanically, she turns her head left from the rigid three-quarter position, to face the camera with a blank and enigmatic stare. She looks out at the spectator as the film's title, *The Queen*, fades in on the shot.

This unmotivated shot works within the logic of the self-contained credit sequence often used by the period film to introduce key narrative themes in an iconographic way. The shot presents Mirren as the Queen borrowing from familiar conventions of public portraiture. In this respect, *The Queen* follows in the footsteps of other historical dramas that validate their representations through the textures of painterly compositions. For example, in *Mrs Brown* the long shots showing Queen Victoria on horse-back in a scene in which she requests a batch of letters from John Brown

Portrait and enigma: Helen Mirren as Elizabeth II in the opening credits of *The Queen*

evoke the Victorian paintings of Sir Edwin Landseer including *Queen Victoria at Osborne House* (1965–67) (Osborne House appears as one of the film's settings, in a bid for authenticity; see McKechnie 2002). This pictorial intertext is seamlessly assimilated into the mise-en-scène as part of the Victorian iconography. As McKechnie argues, the pictorial simply constitutes 'another kind of historicity, which happens to be on a non-verbal level … history films of this kind can open a door to a period too far removed for us to have any personal knowledge of it, by conjuring up a sense of memory through visual imagery' (2001: 111–12). However, when the painterly makes its entrance into a film sequence it can also provisionally suspend the spectator's engagement with the narrative. Its effect is one of (often) kitsch juxtaposition of two different regimes of viewing and two different value systems. 'Tableau' and 'portrait' shots introduce moments of stillness and contemplation into the textures of the filmic, and exploit the public image of historical figures as a commodity fetish, reassuring the audience of the authenticity of the spectacle at the cost of momentarily loosening narrative identification.

When public history is reframed as private history, the over-determined moment of the tableau may become something else: an enigma, posing a hermeneutic task for the film itself to work through. The relationship between spectacle and narrative is thus inverted, as the story told by the heritage film becomes an elaborate caption around the fetish-tableau. In *The Private Lives of Henry VIII* and *The Madness of King George* the tableau is introduced at the beginning of the film, almost as a mythical point of origin for these fictions that seek out the men behind the public image. References to two different paintings bookend *Elizabeth* (see McKechnie 2002), and the plot's effectiveness depends on the spectator recognising intertextual historical images of Elizabeth I in the final sequence. Elaborate costuming, make-up and lighting are used to transform Cate Blanchett into a 'walking tableau'. Elizabeth's mask-like portrait refers to 'the Virgin Queen' persona, which posits an enigma for centuries to come; this enigma motivates the film's focus on transgressive sexual desire and political intrigue. The 'tableau moment' becomes the intrinsic origin of the narrative, while also serving as the extrinsic guarantee of the 'truth' of the illustration provided by the film. Similarly, the tableau-enigma that closes the opening sequence of *The Queen* is highlighted by Mirren's blank stare, her close-up punctuated by a high note at the end of a short musical phrase, like an aural dot stamped upon a question mark drawn by the camera's vertical scrutiny of the royal portrait.

The Queen's blank stare in the royal portrait suggests a playful conceit that encourages the spectator to discover the private person behind the public figure. The film evokes a recognisable heritage universe through long shots of the royal residences of Balmoral in Scotland and Buckingham Palace in London. The two geographical motifs merge into one in the opening establishing shot showing the overcast sky over Buckingham Palace, a prelude to the momentous events that will befall the Windsors, and a piper walking along the imposing line of columns at the Queen's London residence. The Palace interiors (a composite of studio shots) present the everyday life-style of a modern monarchy, discreetly stressing the regimented rituals and routines. In this fortress-like world that encapsulates the continuity of old traditions into the present day, the disruption posed by Diana's actions creeps in through television.

The mise-en-scène of the film is notable for the ubiquitous presence of television sets, which keep the main settings interconnected whilst blurring the boundaries between fictional drama and documentary. The streets outside Buckingham Palace, the headquarters of New Labour, the Blair household, Balmoral and Buckingham Palace, even the Queen's bedchambers, are all spaces repeatedly occupied by characters watching and re-watching footage of Diana during different moments of her life. The impact of Diana, 'the first royal icon raised on and sustained by pop culture' and 'a creation of modern mass media' (Julie Burchill, quoted in Brunt 1998: 69), on public life cannot be underestimated. In contrast with the separation between past and present that results from period reconstruction and the generally linear narratives of the heritage film, images of Diana on television screens punctuate the film (six times in total) with the continuous presentness of the televisual archive. Unlike every other 'real' character in the film, for whom fake news reports and newspaper covers are created using the principal actors, the film uses authentic footage of the Princess of Wales to signal her relentless presence in the media. The snippets of her life on television, continuously played in the wake of her death, constitute the haunting offscreen of the heritage mise-en-scène of The Queen.

The events explored in The Queen correspond to a moment when television had taken over from print media as a means of circulating news, and still dominated over the Internet. From the slightly quaint-looking TV sets in the rooms of the royal servants, to the set planted at the foot of the royal bed, the continuous flow of televisual images into the mise-en-scène of the historical fiction leads to a clash between different temporalities. It is not uncommon for the retro film to incorporate heterogeneous textures and sources (photography, cinema, television) through editing and mise-en-scène, as twentieth-century events and styles become the stuff of the heritage film. In *The Queen* such heterogeneity illustrates a critical view of an institution 'trying desperately to catch up with the times and never quite succeeding' (Edginton 1998: 80) through two different ways of orchestrating the 'historical gaze'. This term, coined by Tom Brown, refers to the relationship between modes of gendered spectacle presupposed by the historical film. According to Brown 'the historical gaze may take different forms, but is essentially the literal embodiment of the standard rhetoric of many historical films, and a means through which the films address the historical knowledge of the spectator' (2008: 163). Focusing on the classical Hollywood film, Brown associates the historical gaze with marked performative gestures, such as eyes that gaze into an imagined distance, or words that seem to address posterity, enacted by actors embodying historical figures. Brown argues that women acquire 'masculine qualities' in moments when they are positioned in vantage points that command spectacular vistas over public events. Such moments allow for 'the inscription of the "big history" to come and the character's recognition of his/her place in it' (2008: 165). Although the acting styles of the contemporary historical film cannot be readily equated to those of the cinema from the Hollywood studio era, it can be suggested that the notion of the historical gaze is productively extended to the reframing of (internal) personal dilemmas as (external) historical conflicts in *The Queen* and, by extension, the heritage film.

Key turning points in the narrative are signalled by Mirren's performance, as the Queen gradually realises the challenges posed by the public reaction to Diana's death. In a scene that presents her writing in her diary, she lifts her eyes and looks offscreen, allowing a pause for reflection. A strings theme played in minor key that previously underscored her phone conversation with Blair now draws attention to this conventional gesture, which gives the spectator an insight into the subtle changes the character is undergoing. This gesture reappears twice: at the end of the second act, as the Queen insistently looks ahead, lost in thought, while strolling alongside her mother at Balmoral and again in a medium shot of her in

Meaningful gestures: historical conflict as personal dilemma in *The Queen*

the library. In the latter scene, her figure is melancholically side-lit and appears sharply defined in the foreground against the blurred waist-down figure of Charles, who stands in the background congratulating his mother on her decision to return to London. The careful gradation and repetition of a performative gesture across different moments of the film not only directs the spectator's attention to the character's change of heart: more significantly, it also alludes to the inevitability of historical events already transformed into heritage.

The historical gaze attributed to the Queen can be compared to two moments in the film in which Diana is shown 'looking back': a glance in freeze-frame included in the first montage of news footage of Diana, ten minutes into the film, is later matched by a single shot of Diana's glance, inserted after the thunderous row of applause that follows Lord Spencer's eulogy during the funeral sequence in the final part of the film. The representation of the Queen's gaze clashes with this figuration of a different type of look that arises from television's role in constructing the Diana myth. As Jenny Kitzinger points out:

> Part of Diana's appeal lay in gesture and movement. Her famous 'look' could not be fully captured in a still photograph. Its 'flirta-tious' effect lay in eye movement, the intense glance followed by the shy look away. Her attraction lay not in 'posing' but in 'spon-

taneity'. It is no coincidence that standard formal paintings of her were said to appear insipid. In this sense Princess Diana was neither 'attractive' nor even simply photogenic, she was, above all, 'telegenic'. (1998: 76)

Diana's last enigmatic glance at the camera becomes a moment frozen in time, inscribing the Princess as a haunting presence through the constant replay on television screens. In the funeral sequence, several layers of representation coalesce: actual footage of the crowds outside Westminster Abbey and of Lord Spencer's eulogy combines with shots involving the principal performers. The effect of this docudrama technique is a seamless reconstruction of a historical event, the Princess's funeral, as a heritage narrative. However, whereas the story told by *The Queen* answers the question posed by the tableau shot of Elizabeth II in the opening sequence, Diana's glance remains an enigma that haunts the margins of the film and raises the question of a potentially different, but unrealised narrative of monarchy.

Significantly, the resolution of the drama arrives when the Queen enters the televisual space through her address to the nation. The sequence of the Queen's speech faithfully reconstructs the record of public history, bringing closure to a week of crisis. However, Mirren's performance also captures the provisional nature of this resolution. It has been argued that the content of the original broadcast points to the tensions underlying different meanings of nation, more specifically the 'nation-as-Establishment' as opposed to the 'nation-as-people' (see Edington 1998: 80). This tension is compellingly brought to the surface in the mise-en-scène of the Queen standing inside Buckingham Palace while double-framed by the monitor screen. She poses as formally for television as she did for the official portrait, seemingly impervious to the qualities of closeness, communication and spontaneity demanded by the medium – qualities which made Diana a truly telegenic presence and, it is suggested, make Tony Blair a shrewd politician.

The Queen turns the tables on the opposition of history versus heritage once more in its closing sequence. During a last meeting with a smug Blair, the Queen retorts that he should prepare himself for public opinion changing 'suddenly, and without warning'. By stressing the changeability of historical narratives in a time of 24/7 media coverage, *The Queen* calls on its audience to evaluate the momentous events of 1997 from the perspective of 2006. In this respect, the film functions not as a critique of the Royal Family but as a reflection on the role of an institution cemented in history and tradition at a time of epochal change. In spite of its largely sympathetic portrait of Blair, *The Queen* finally endows Elizabeth II's historical gaze with an understated superiority, allowing the heritage narrative to capture the disenchantment with the present. This can be read as a conservative retreat into the values of permanence and continuity embodied by the monarch. As one reviewer remarked, under the trappings of the monarchy film *The Queen* is awash with a 'sweet nostalgia for the golden age of Labour landslides' (Christopher 2006), which tinges the looking back on a unique moment of spontaneous performance of citizenship prompted by the rise of a newly elected leader and the demise of a celebrity princess. At the same time, this exercise of looking back is arguably framed by New Labour's losses, and especially by Blair's highly unpopular decision to enter the wars in Afghanistan and Iraq (see Leggott 2008: 3). The idea of national unity traditionally sustained by the mise-en-scène of heritage thus emerges as a rhetorical construction subject to continuous interrogation and redefinition in the age of media spin and post-devolution Britain. Ultimately, the sharp sense of irony in *The Queen* arises, not just from the spectacle of the past that fails to fall into step with the present, but also from a present (the period of New Labour government, reframed as the past) that failed to live up to its promise.

The heritage film and the return of the national

The Queen begs the question of what we mean when we talk about 'the nation' in cinema, television and popular culture. Can the film reflect the British nation faithfully at a specific turning point of its history? Are the crowds gathered outside the sea of flowers deposited at the gates of Buckingham Palace representative of the *whole* nation? As we saw at the beginning of this chapter, the heritage film has been accused of mythologising (and misrepresenting) the national past via a stable and conservative iconography. *The Queen* does not escape this charge. The Scotland represented in the sequences at Balmoral appears not only as a landscape out of history (see McArthur 1982), but also as a healing space where the Queen can find room to express her feelings. Writing on Scotland and the heritage film after devolution, Sarah Neely interrogates the representation offered by *Mrs Brown*; she points out that '*Mrs Brown*, like many of the early heritage films, is structured as journey to a "foreign" place that leads to self-discovery and an exploration of issues of class and gender' (2005: 244). This statement is equally applicable to the events chronicled in *The Queen*, where Elizabeth II insists on remaining in Balmoral to escape public pressure and to perform her duties as a grandmother, rather than as a monarch. As noted by Colin McArthur and others, the Scottish landscape has been used in film to elicit a sense of romantic abandon and return to nature, often presented as a refuge from the conflicts provoked by urban modernity. In *The Queen*, the expanses of the Highlands bring moments of visual relief by opening up the constrained interior settings of the royal residences to spectacular aerial views. The Scottish landscape performs as the backdrop for the 'encounter' between the Queen, implausibly stranded alone with her jeep in a remote part of her Scottish estate, and a majestic stag. The digitally altered shots of the stag are reminiscent of the popular iconography of Scotland ranging from Victorian painting (for example, Landseer's *The Monarch of the Glen*, 1851) to contemporary advertising (the stag is the logo for the commercial brand of whisky Glenfiddich). The perfect illusion created by the shot/reverse-shot sequence of Mirren facing the stag constitutes another, unexpected instance of the historical gaze, not least for the powerful ideological cliché it encapsulates. Not unlike the friendship between Queen Victoria and John Brown in *Mrs Brown*, the magical encounter between a tearful Queen and the quasi-mythical animal conveys Scotland's healing power. In a rare spontaneous gesture, the Queen, aware of the nearby presence of hunters led by her husband, warns the stag to take flight. This encounter ambiguously conflates a popular version of the events referred to in the film – Diana as the victim, a 'hunted animal' irrationally pursued by the press – with a reinterpretation of them: the Queen herself as a creature stalked by unbearable pressures.

In the turbulent negotiations of Englishness at stake in *The Queen*, alternative signifiers of nation are mobilised to provide a temporary escape from pressing political concerns. Scotland functions as a location that is crucial to the private trajectory of the film's central character, but peripheral to the discourses of political power. The film thus follows the steps of earlier British heritage films, such as *Chariots of Fire*, by looking at Scotland 'from the outside (or rather from the metropolitan English centre) associating it with the "natural" and the "primitive"' (Hill 1997: 245). Whilst in *Elizabeth* and *Elizabeth: The Golden Age* Scotland figures as a focus of political and military insurgency that must be quashed in order to affirm the authority of the monarch, in *Mrs Brown* and *The Queen* Scotland is a space of mourning where the Queen is able to give in to her feelings but also to assume her historical 'destiny'. The depiction of the Windsors at home in the rural Scottish landscape (the Queen and the Royal Family are depicted picnicking, driving, hiking and stalking stags) does not fail to stress the opposition with the idealised vision of white English femininity represented by Diana: urban, glamorous and cosmopolitan. The appropriation of Scottishness betrays the structures of colonisation that sustain heritage's myth-making, even as the horizon of the past gets closer to the present within the flexible limits of the heritage film.

The scene of the Queen with the stag was widely used for promotional purposes in television broadcasts, especially in the wake of the film's success at the Academy Awards. Such reductive iconography of nation clearly contributed to the international success of Frears and Morgan's film. This was confirmed by a string of awards, including the Volpi Cup for Best Actress at the 2006 Venice Film Festival, the 2007 Bafta Awards for Best Film and Best Actress and, most importantly for the commercial performance of the film, the Oscar for Best Actress awarded to Mirren. Mirren's public appearances as part of the marketing campaign constitute an unexpected point of conflation between institutional power and popular media culture. In her much-commented-upon acceptance speech at the 2007 Academy Awards ceremony, Mirren dedicated her Oscar to Elizabeth II and saluted 'her courage and her consistency'. She closed her speech with a theatrical 'ladies and gentlemen, I give you the Queen'. Whether this was a bid to make a speech of 'historical importance'[15] or a mere marketing ploy, it is worth noting how two institutions – British cinema and the British monarchy – reinforced each other's momentary resurgence in the global media. Viewed positively, this could be understood as an imaginative exploitation of cultural synergies accomplished by the continuous upgrading of well-trodden generic formulas. Conversely, a more cynical reading of Mirren's performance at the Oscars may suggest parallelisms with a former 'the British are coming!' moment (after Colin Welland's famous words upon receiving the Academy Award for Best Screenplay in 1982 for his work on *Chariots of Fire*), indicative of a cyclical surge of jingoism that obscures the realities affecting British cinema as a fragile film industry in perpetual state of identity crisis.

The international success achieved by *The Queen* suggests that global audiences continue to be fascinated by the cultural idiosyncrasies and accessible iconography of heritage Englishness. The national is subject to a perpetual return, and yet it is open to debate whether this should be viewed as a back-door strategy of resistance, or an orchestrated campaign designed to keep national industries on the global spotlight. We shall turn to this question in the next chapter, looking at the larger context of the heritage film in Europe.

Notes

1 Independent filmmaker Alex Cox called it 'condescending propaganda' and a 'war-friendly – and essentially mid-Atlantic – version of British film history' in a column published in *The Guardian* (2007); Robert Murphy dismissed it as 'ill-informed and dull' (2009: 2).

2 For a full analysis of the production and reception history of *Chariots of Fire*, see the comprehensive account by James Chapman (see 2005: 270–98).

3 The sequence was actually shot at Eton after Cambridge University refused permission to film in the college grounds, allegedly because the script portrayed the University as an antisemitic institution (see Chapman 2005: 277).

4 See, for instance, Hipsky (1994), Dave (1997), Hill (1999). Also, LeMahieu (1990) prefigures the terms of the debate.

5 In an incendiary piece published in *The Sunday Times* in 1988, right-wing historian Norman Stone attacked independent British films such as *The Last of England* (Derek Jarman, 1987) and *Sammy and Rosie Get Laid* (Stephen Frears, 1987) that rebelled against the status quo of the Thatcher era, while praising the period dramas *Passage to India* and *A Room with a View*. Stone's intervention further polarised the debates. For a full account, see Monk (2002).

6 The devolution of power to the Scottish Parliament and the Welsh Assembly in the late 1990s presupposes the entrance in a new 'post-devolution Britain', which fundamentally alters the political analysis of British cinema. See Blandford (2007).

7   See Chapman (2005) for an extended analysis of *The Private Life of Henry VIII*.

8   For a detailed study of the distribution and exhibition history of these films in the USA, see Street (2002).

9   With an estimated budget of approximately $7.5 million, *Howards End* took $25 million in the USA, see Higson (2003: 156) and Hill (1999: 79).

10 This much-cited phrase originated in a cartoon authored by Alan Parker that lampooned the emphasis on costume and set design in the Merchant Ivory films as well as their imaginary audience of upper-middle-class consumers.

11 The output of Channel Four Films included decade-defining works such as *My Beautiful Laundrette* (Stephen Frears, 1985) and *Distant Voices, Still Lives*, which worked both as theatrical releases and quality television programming. For a useful account of the evolving relations between Channel Four and film production, see Brooke (n.d.).

12 On the television scriptwriter as author, see Cardwell (2005).

13 McKechnie (2002) also notes that the production of *Elizabeth* (the film started shooting shortly after Diana's death) was touched by the prevailing atmosphere after the event.

14 I am referring here to Geraghty's categories, the 'star-as-celebrity', 'star-as-professional' and 'star-as-performer' (see 2000: 188–96).

15 As suggested by Simon Mayo and Mark Kermode in a special report on the Academy Awards (BBC, 26 February 2007).

2   PRODUCTION CYCLES AND CULTURAL SIGNIFICANCE: A EUROPEAN HERITAGE FILM?

The debates on the heritage film have spilled over and beyond the borders of British cinema. This critical term has been used to conceptualise other national historical imaginaries that have become visible in the international distribution circuits especially since the mid-1990s. This chapter considers the possibility of a *European* heritage film in light of two factors: on the one hand, since the 1990s the heritage film has been targeted at international as well as national audiences; on the other, supra-national funding and collaboration between international partners (including American invest-ment in the production and distribution of European films) has promoted the generic consistency of national iconographies and the production of heritage films. Viewed from the perspective of competition and collabora-tion, the heritage film has contributed to the branding of national cinemas as part of a new cosmopolitan culture aimed at global consumption. The main case study in this chapter is Christian Carion's *Joyeux Noël*, a his-torical co-production purposefully created and marketed as a 'European' film. Focusing on the true account of a truce during World War I, *Joyeux Noël* capitalises on the potential of traumatic history to promote a shared heritage.

The heritage film in Europe: state intervention and national identity

As we saw in the previous chapter, the heritage critique has tended to present British period dramas as a middlebrow phenomenon associated with a conservative turn in 1980s British cinema. In spite of the national specificity of the original debates, the heritage critique has subsequently been adopted in international contexts. Scholars working on various national cinemas have found the term useful in the discussion of modern historical films, costume romances, classic adaptations and biopics with period settings; that is, films that combine generic appeal with literary and/or historical credentials. Indeed, from the late 1990s onwards the heritage film has started to function as a critical umbrella term for almost any type of costume film that subscribes to styles of picturesque realism. It has been applied retrospectively to films that achieved international recognition after becoming domestic hits. In an early attempt at 'europeanising' the term, Richard Dyer suggests the French film *Jean de Florette* (Claude Berri, 1986), the Spanish film *Belle Époque* (Fernando Trueba, 1992) and the Danish production *Babettes gæstebud* (*Babette's Feast*, Gabriel Axel, 1987) as examples of 'conventional filmic narrative style, with the pace and tone of "(European) art cinema" but without its symbolisms and personal directorial voices' (1995: 204). Likewise, the Italian-French period dramas *Nuovo Cinema Paradiso* (*Cinema Paradiso*, Giuseppe Tornatore, 1988) and *Il Postino* (*The Postman*, Michael Radford, 1994) proved that European films could do well in world markets if promoted as popular art films with strong generic elements (romantic comedy and melodrama). In content and form these films come across as nostalgic, not so much because the past evoked is necessarily embellished, but because it is presented as discursively stable and clearly separated from the present by flashbacks and the markers of period reconstruction. Memory and individual experience, often presented through the point of view of children or marginalised characters, are used to introduce historical events. A strong sense of place, which arises from evocative landscapes, geographical landmarks, local customs and recognisable (though often clichéd) character types, locates these films within specific national imaginaries. These elements are cemented by narratives that minimise ambiguity and seek instead to elicit an emotional response to character-driven storytelling structured around satisfying dynamics of conflict and resolution.

At the turn of the 1990s these national heritage films were embraced by international audiences in search of the pleasures of cultural authenticity without the perceived demands of the art film. This not only raises concerns about representation (how a national culture is portrayed in fiction films) but also about *representativeness* (how central the heritage film is to Italian, Spanish or French film cultures). These two issues have become particularly prominent in the changing landscape of European cinemas, not least because the heritage film's growing international visibility in the 1980s paralleled the decline of 1960s art cinemas, suggesting a return to classical European film styles (see Vincendeau 1998: 446). At the same time, the heritage film's middlebrow mode of address suppresses or tones down the idiosyncrasies of taste and locality that characterise lowbrow genres. For some critics, this is tantamount to a homogeneisation of form and content in European cinemas complicit with disturbing acts of cultural erasure. Writing in 1997, Geoffrey Nowell-Smith argues:

> The current crop of heritage films is evidence of a worrying trend in European cinema. It is not just that most of them have little critical edge and that they are content to replicate an image of a nice past whose occasional nastiness we can complacently claim to have outgrown. More dangerous for the long-term future of European cinema is the temptation they provide to retreat into a kind of upmarket Disneyfication of Europe as a celluloid theme park from which the discontents of modernity have been comfortably banished. (1997: 766)

This critique implicitly locates the true originality and significance of European cinemas in the traditions of socially committed cinema and modernist aesthetics, disregarding what Rosalind Galt calls *la belle image* (2006: 9–10). Galt uses this phrase, which literally means 'the beautiful image', to refer to the postmodern spectacle of the past conveyed through the coupling of romance and landscape imagery in the heritage film. The latter is especially prominent in the aforementioned *Cinema Paradiso* and *Il Postino*, which achieved wide circulation as Italian heritage films in the early 1990s. With regard to international distribution Galt notes that such films frequently seem 'to lose whatever edge a national narrative might involve and to appear to foreign audiences as just another pretty European indie' (2006: 8). However, Galt argues that the 'pretty' images of Italianness delivered by these films (which Nowell-Smith's modernist critique sees as empty and affectless) express a melodramatic sensibility that is evocative of a specific national history. She argues that these popular films engage with a moment of political possibility (the immediate post-war period) that

is relived in the context of the national political crisis that led to the col-
lapse of the Italian First Republic in 1992 (2006). The juxtaposition of two
historically situated moments, both in the past and the present, allows
the picturesque landscapes of the Italian heritage film to become far more
than just a vehicle for escapist nostalgia. For Galt, *la belle image*, or the
'prettiness of Italian cinema'[1] is symptomatic of a traumatic national past
acknowledged through the play of temporality that allows the spectator to
contemplate that lost moment of (emotional, social and political) potential. Her incisive analysis of the popular Italian period film of the 1990s as a
'look back on an irreversible history' (2006: 43) is central to understanding
the political potential of heritage spectacle in European cinemas during a
key period of territorial and political reconfiguration.

The late 1980s and early 1990s constitute a moment of social, economic and political upheaval which would not leave any of the main film
producing nations in Europe untouched. The fall of the Berlin Wall in 1989
and the subsequent revolutions in the East-European Communist states,
the wars in the Balkans following the dissolution of Yugoslavia in 1991,
and the break-up of the Soviet Union in 1992 effected a radical change
in European geopolitical relations. As Luisa Rivi has noted, the European
states took steps towards the construction of a supra-national entity,
the European Union, which forged new and diverse connections at sub-
national (micro-regionalism) and supra-national (macro-regionalism)
levels; these changes have necessitated a significant rearticulation of the
conventional meanings of the nation-state and national identity that take
into consideration the polycentric post-1989 map of Europe, 'where multiple powers at the local, national and global levels coexist within, as well
as create, a supranational framework' (2007: 3). As Rivi also points out,
the persistence of the nation-state depends upon its rearticulation in ways
that recognise not only its plural and multiple identities within and beyond
its limits, but also that actively engage with the legacies of imperialism
and colonisation. Not surprisingly, the representation of key events of
twentieth-century history is a recurrent theme across the various European
national cinemas, yet it is one that, more often than not, is fraught with
ideological tensions and political suspicion.

The end of Cold War bi-polarism coincided with a cultural turn to the
study of collective memory as an antidote to the hegemonic, and occassionally repressive, role performed by official histories. In this respect, the

British heritage film debate is echoed in a number of national contexts across Europe via the replication of arguments about institutional rather than historical or industrial frameworks. The emphasis on sedate pictorialism (*la belle image*) and individual stories, often set against the backdrop of turbulent times, gets associated with reactionary attempts to conjure up reassuring images of national identity in the face of seismic changes. Thus, in France, the term *lieu de mémoire*, coined by Pierre Nora in his seminal multi-volume work *Les lieux de mémoire* (published between 1986 and 1992), has entered the French language to denote symbolic sites or events (the literal meaning of *lieux*) that belong to the heritage of a given community and are cemented in public memory over time (see Greene 1999). France's cohesive sense of national identity had been undermined by the deep wounds left by the Nazi occupation of the country during most of World War II, the Algerian war of decolonisation in the early 1960s and the failed revolution of May 1968. The need to recuperate the *lieux de mémoire* that could ensure the continuity of the national past becomes especially acute at a time of progressive disintegration of narratives of nation and empire.

French cinema scholars in Britain were quick to point out this backdrop to establish parallels between the heritage film in Britain and the *nostalgia film* in 1980s France. For Phil Powrie (1997), the search for traditional national identities emerges through a strong regional iconography in the diptych *Jean de Florette* and *Manon des sources* (both France/Switzerland/Italy co-productions, directed by Claude Berri in 1986) and the affirmation of European culture in the literary adaptation *Un Amour de Swann* (*Swann in Love*, Volker Schlöndorff, 1984). These films evoke literary, painterly and musical landmarks, constructing period spectacles suffused with a sense of melancholia for lost times. In the context of French film history the popular costume drama of the 1980s is viewed as a throwback to the 1950s 'tradition of quality' (*la tradition de la qualité*), a mode of filmmaking that has consistently been relegated to a mere preamble to the cinematic modernism brought about by the filmmakers associated with the 1960s French New Wave (although the period is being reassessed; see Hayward 2008).

The 1980s costume drama thus would posit a new brand of quality film (*la nouvelle qualité française*): a prestigious but 'popular' cultural cinema that is also an example of a top-down state-supported cinema more in evidence in France than in Britain. The state funding policies of the 1980s brought the genre into close alignment with the political interests of the socialist government of François Mitterrand, who made dealing with the legacy of the Occupation and the colonial wars a priority of his mandate (1981–95) (see Austin 2008: 168–70). Under Jack Lang, first as Minister of Culture and then of Education, generous funding was allocated to prestige projects such as the co-production *Danton* (Andrzej Wajda, 1983) as well as the cycle of adaptations of Marcel Pagnol's novels, including the extremely popular films by Yves Robert, *La Gloire de mon père* (*My Father's Glory*, 1990) and *Le Château de ma mère* (*My Mother's Castle*, 1990), which followed in the footsteps of the success of *Jean de Florette* and *Manon des sources*. Another heritage strand exploits the combination of epic romance and colonial backdrops. In *Fort Saganne* (Alain Corneau, 1984) and *Indochine* (*Indochina*, Régis Wargnier, 1992) end-of-empire narratives deliver the assets of French quality, including the allure of the mature stars Gérard Depardieu and Catherine Deneuve. Depardieu's revived stardom in the 1990s is particularly associated to the French heritage film. The resounding success of the much-loved *Cyrano de Bergerac* (Jean-Paul Rappenau, 1990) earned him the Best Actor Award at the 1990 Cannes Film Festival and the French *César* for Best Actor in 1991, and contributed decisively to his status as a national symbol of international magnitude (see Vincendeau 2000).

National symbol: Gérard Depardieu in *Cyrano de Bergerac*

By the mid-1990s the French heritage film (including the *film en costumes*, or *film de patrimoine*, as well as the classic literary adaptation) moved centre-stage not only as an example of a successful cultural export, but also as a flagship of the politics of 'cultural exception'. In the acrimonious GATT (Global Agreement on Tariffs and Trades) negotiations of 1992–94, Claude Berri's classic literary adaptation *Germinal* (1993) stood out against the backdrop of the French-American dispute over the status of cultural products in international trade agreements. A prestige film based on a key text in the national curriculum (Émile Zola's 1885 novel of the same name), *Germinal,* like *Cyrano de Bergerac,* enshrined French heritage in terms of its linguistic specificity, high production values and a star cast that included Depardieu, Miou-Miou and folk-music icon Rénaud. *Germinal* is an example of cinema as a direct expression of national history and values, especially in its idealised representation of the historical role played by the political left. These credentials symbolise national cinema as a product that, in the stance adopted by the French government in the negotiations, needed to be considered as a cultural exception to general trade regulations and therefore protected via 'special handling' in the form of subsidies and screen quotas. This position antagonised the American delegation at the GATT negotiations. Saluted as a 'quasi-national undertaking' (Cousins 1999: 27), *Germinal* benefitted from a broad spectrum of institutional support not only at the level of production but also of distribution and exhibition, including its promotion in schools. In box office and press coverage terms it was a film event in France that notoriously faced up to the massive global release of Steven Spielberg's *Jurassic Park* (1993). However, its value as a political statement was tempered by its position as a reactionary, nationalist response to the perceived threat of American cultural imperialism. Russell Cousins, for instance, notes its sanitised take on Zola's novel and the vacuity of its melodramatic portrait of the mining community. For him *Germinal*, as a heritage film, constitutes an anodyne account of French social history and an example of an apolitical aesthetics of spectacle that serves 'an ideology validating consensus rather than conflict' (1999: 35). The heritage film was thus instrumentalised as a symbol of the dualism of culture versus commodity that defined *l'exception française* ('the French exception') in the 1993 GATT negotiations; a position that proved moot when France subsequently softened its stance and signed deals with American companies. The *Germinal* controversy is symptomatic of the use of national cultural products as a form of 'resistance' in the face of 'both continuing Americanization and encroaching Europeanization' (Elizabeth Ezra and Sue Harris, quoted in Rivi 2007: 57).

The reception and critical analysis of the French heritage film becomes more complex in the context of the strong auteur tradition that has traditionally privileged personal (that is, director-driven) films over genre productions. At the turn of the 1960s, French New Wave cinema exported the notion of the *auteur* (according to which the director is credited as 'author' of a film), which would become a mainstay of European cinema at large. As noted earlier, the promotion of the auteur was partly built on a symbolic break with a long-standing tradition of quality, which integrated popular costume films and literary adaptations. In a contentious move, young critic and soon-to-be filmmaker François Truffaut published his polemical article 'A Certain Tendency in French Cinema' in *Cahiers du cinéma* in 1954. In this piece, Truffaut demolished the script-driven literary adaptations of the tradition of quality and championed instead a cinema of auteurs. His intervention posits a significant precedent to the critical split between auteur and heritage cinema. The lingering impact of this critique can be observed in the use of derogative terms such as *académisme* ('academicism' or formal unadventurousness) and 'new tradition of quality' that continue to be applied to the modern costume film in France and elsewhere in Europe (see, for example, de Baecque 1992). As Ginette Vincendeau perceptively notes (2005: 139), the defence in the pages of *Cahiers du cinéma* of costume dramas signed by directors with auteur standing – Patrice Chéreau's *La Reine Margot* (*Queen Margot*, 1994) and *Gabrielle* (2005); Éric Rohmer's *L'Anglaise et le duc* (*The Lady and the Duke*, 2001); and especially Olivier Assayas' family saga *Les Destinées sentimentales* (*Sentimental Destinies*, 2000) – betrays the absence of a systematic critique informed by genre and gender approaches that tackles the heritage film as an identifiable stylistic practice.

The above examples suggest a fruitful terrain for the study of the intersection of the spectacular *film en costumes* with varied auteur practices and oppositional reflections on national identity. As Julianne Pidduck has noted, the operatic *La Reine Margot*, a monarchy film that depicts the Huguenot massacre in the sixteenth century, 'personalises' and 'intensifies' violent acts of history, making them 'of the present' (2005: 61–2). The grandeur and immediacy of its blood-suffused imagery attested its political relevance, as the film was read by part of the French press as a visceral response to the images of genocide that emerged from the Balkans and Rwanda in the 1990s. For feminist critics like Geneviève Sellier, however, the counterpoint to the film's reponsive stance towards history is the sexual stereotyping of its central female character and her lack of political agency (see Vincendeau 2001b; Pidduck 2005). Spectacle and political reflection also meet in the woman-centred melodramas *La Veuve de St Pierre* (*The Widow of St Pierre*, Patrice Leconte, 2000) and *Saint-Cyr* (*The King's Daughters*, Patricia Mazuy, 2000), two films whose approach to French history from peripheral and marginalised feminine positions are indicative of the political potential of the heritage genre in France and the vitality of women's cinema.

France's key symbolic and economic role at the centre of European cinema continues, to a large extent, to be attached to its support of home-grown and international film auteurs through funding frameworks set up by the Centre National de Cinématographie (CNC) (see Jäckel 2007). However, European national cinemas experienced a decisive turn to popular genres in the 1990s. This phenomenon, one of the by-products of globalisation, is especially remarkable in the case of the period dramas emerging from Eastern European countries. As noted by Tim Bergfelder, the return to traditional conceptions of the national is especially noticeable in film-producing countries 'that feel beleaguered in their political or cultural identity, and in countries which see themselves as either economically excluded or culturally independent from the developments of central and Western Europe' (2005: 319). As the old geopolitical bipolarism has given way to uneven economic integration into the larger structures of Europe, the links between the heritage film, state support and the 'teaching of the nation' to new generations of cinemagoers have become increasingly important in the cultural re-formulation of the national in East Central Europe. The period film in general, and the epic in particular, need to be examined in contexts of state intervention that seeks to promote nation-building versions of the historical past. The historical super-production boom in Poland, especially large-scale epics based on literary classics like *Pan Tadeusz* (*Pan Tadeusz: The Last Foray in Lithuania*, Andrzej Wajda, 1999) and *Ogniem i mieczem* (*With Fire and Sword*, Jerzy Hoffman, 1999), are, according to Dina Iordanova part of a 'concerted heritage management effort' that harks back to the 1960s and has accelerated in the 1990s

(2003: 49). As she and Ewa Mazierska (2001) both note, this trend leaves little room for alternative representations of national identity.

A different example of this state-endorsed heritage cinema, the European super-production *Sibirskij Tsiryulnik* (*The Barber of Siberia*, Nikita Mikhalkov, 1998) brought together international funds and personnel for a large scale film that taps into the iconography of Tsarist Russia, as seen through the eyes of American traveller Jane Callahan (Julia Ormond). *The Barber of Siberia* is a sumptuous Russian, French, Italian and Czech co-production, largely shot at the Barrandov Studios near Prague. The film was designed to compete with Hollywood blockbusters: at the time in which it was made, it claimed the highest budget ($46 million) for a European production. Funding came through private initiatives from Eastern and Western Europe (led by director-producer Nikita Mikhalkov through his company TriTe and the French producer Michel Seydoux, head of Caméra One). Ormond plays a wilful American gold-digger who, during her travels in late nineteenth-century Russia, meets and falls in love with cadet Tolstoi (Oleg Menshikov), a romantic and fiercely individualistic hero. The film alternates between English and Russian as befits a cast of British and Russian stars, and unfolds as a romantic drama structured around lavish set pieces including duels, military parades, a grand ball and a tense dénouement during a performance of the opera *The Marriage of Figaro*. 'Russianness', as a romantic idiom reminiscent of past film representations such as *Dr Zhivago* (David Lean, 1965), is filtered through the point of view of the non-Russian characters as an excessive spectacle of heightened emotions that mixes comedy and melodrama. An exercise in self-exoticism, which appeals to patriotic pride and celebrates an essential 'Russian character', the film was advertised as a national event and enjoyed a première at the Kremlin Palace of Congress. The publicity campaign that accompanied the film's release included the launch of an associated vodka brand and a perfume range, helping to transform *The Barber of Siberia* into an extended commercial for the 'product Russia' (Beumers 2000: 201). The mobilisation of heritage functioned to support an unreconstructed national identity that promotes a nostalgic image of the pre-Soviet past for times of economic uncertainty.

As these examples suggest, the critique of the heritage film in Europe has largely concentrated on the conservative retreat into national iconographies at a time of socio-political instability. New cycles of literary adaptations and historical epics have arisen at a moment when fears of the cultural effects of globalisation (often equalled to the Americanisation of culture) have reignited a protective 'fortress Europe' mentality. In the early 1990s, European policy-makers sought to build protective walls around the audiovisual sector (in the form of screening quotas and subsidies) in order to shelter it from free-market pressures. *Germinal* and *The Barber of Siberia* received ample institutional endorsement that elevated them to national events but they failed to achieve comparable international impact (in spite of framing the narrative from the perspective of American characters, *The Barber of Siberia* did not secure theatrical distribution in the US). The heritage super-productions of the 1990s highlight not only the difficulty for a large-scale popular European cinema not in the English-language to 'conquer' the international markets, but also the problematic definition of the popular when co-opted by nation-building institutional ideologies.

The heritage critique needs to take into account the new conditions of production. Nation-based, state-subsidised film industries have become increasingly open to transnational ventures shaped by the allocation of supra-national funds, and the intervention of private funders across borders (with de-regulated television stations now playing major roles in film production). The European heritage film since the mid-1990s has become the product of complex economic arrangements that involve public subsidies and private funding. This includes arrangements between film production companies and television stations; for example, *Germinal, Pan Tadeusz* and *The Barber of Siberia* were partly funded by the French media conglomerate Canal+. In an increasingly fluid map of international co-operation and economic opportunities in a global market, the opposition of Hollywood versus Europe has become increasingly meaningless. Hollywood studios operate as decentralised entities that obtain the bulk of their revenue from overseas investments through alliances with independent producers and partnerships with foreign investors (see Balio 1998). The genres and themes that constitute the heritage film (the historical epic, the literary adaptation, or the artist's biopic) thus fulfil the need for a type of mainstream popular film that mobilises a shared iconography recognisable across national borders while also capitalising on cultural difference as a commercial asset. With this premise in mind, the next two sections look at significant examples of the heritage film as a transnational genre, that is, the outcome of co-production trends in Europe and the industrial practices of global Hollywood. The contention here is that the understanding of these de-centralised networks is key to the analysis of a changing heritage aesthetic that draws creatively on transnational resources and a shared European history. These economic and industrial structures favour character-driven genre films with a strong investment in cultural recognition and emotion, rather than in the specificity of national experience.

Supra-national funding and shared histories

In Western and Eastern Europe alike, the 1990s saw a 'crisis of identity in an era that marks the end of national cinemas' (Iordanova 1999: 47). The reconfiguration of national production in Europe took place within new frameworks of international co-operation. In particular, European policy has been a motor in the construction of a supra-national space that fosters the interaction of cultural agents operating within and beyond nation-states. The introduction of the Television Without Frontiers Directive (the new audio-visual policy launched in 1989 to promote a single European audiovisual space), the MEDIA programme,[2] and Eurimages (the Council of Europe's pan-European fund), are some of the measures that have radically affected the make-up of European film (see Rivi 2007). Initially subscribed to by twelve member states, and currently integrating 33 countries, the Eurimages fund has sought to stimulate co-operation between partners with high and low production potential, and makes a particular effort to sustain projects that originate in member states with a low cinematic output (see Jäckel 2003). This system of fund allocation has not been free from criticism as it is perceived to have created inequalities that have favoured smaller member states.[3] These schemes are guided by a cultural remit to 'support works which uphold the values that are part and parcel of European identity' (Council of Europe Forum, quoted in Jäckel 2003: 76), thus bestowing on co-produced films a 'previously nonexistent seal of Europeanness' (Rivi 2007: 63).

In practice, these measures acknowledge transnational arrangements as an unavoidable way forward for a sustainable, post-1989 European cinema, since most national markets are not sufficiently large or economically healthy for films to recoup production costs domestically. In this new post-national map of European cinema, the heritage film has emerged as a type of film strongly favoured by investors and funding bodies alike. Its appeal to a common cultural heritage makes it likely to export well across national borders as an upmarket product with the potential to reach wide audiences. However, cultural and economic interests do not always go hand in hand. Piecemeal funding from diverse sources and complicated co-production regulations often necessitate production and casting decisions that undermine the artistic coherence of the films. *La Putain du roi* (*The King's Whore*, Axel Corti, 1990), an Austrian, French, Italian and British co-production with an eccentric multi-national cast playing French and Italian characters in accented English, has been cited as the first 'European' entry at the Cannes Film Festival, where it received a poor critical response (see Halle 2002: 33). European heritage films like this one often invoked the derisive sobriquet 'Europudding', a term used to refer to multi-national films that erase cultural specificity in favour of strategic casting and language decisions.

The European Convention on Cinematographic Co-production issued by the Council in 1992 was set up to upgrade and streamline earlier co-production arrangements. Likewise, the Eurimages fund, which originally requested the participation of a minimum of three member states, started to encourage bilateral films in 1998. These changes indicated a turn towards the co-financing rather than the co-production of films, which opened up new possibilities for collaboration with no cultural strings attached. The Convention has introduced modes of financial contribution that demand a financial input of between 10 and 25 per cent of the budget from minority partners without requiring equivalent artistic or technical participation. This circumvents quota-meeting artistic decisions (in terms of choices of personnel) that may otherwise undermine the credibility of the production (see Rivi 2007), as it was arguably the case with *The King's Whore*.

A similar turn has been registered in European regional funding bodies. A notable case is the Nordic Film and TV Fund (NFTF), originally established to support production in Scandinavian countries. The NFTF switched its early emphasis on co-productions with Nordic content to the stimulation of a Nordic space of co-operation that presupposes a shared culture of circulation and reception, a phenomenon studied by Mette Hjort (2005). Since the mid-1990s flexible models of collaboration created through co-financing regimes have been accompanied by a new tolerance, or even appetite for cultural hybridity on the part of Scandinavian audiences. A

A Nordic heritage?: Maria Bonnevie in *I Am Dina*

striking example is *Jag är Dina* (*I Am Dina*, 2002), a co-production between Sweden, Norway, Denmark, France and Germany, directed by Danish director Ole Bornedal, adapted from a canonical novel by Norwegian author Herbjørg Wassmo, and featuring a multi-national cast that included Maria Bonnevie (Swedish), Mads Mikkelsen (Danish), Gérard Depardieu (French) and Christopher Eccleston (British), all speaking in accented English. The film's success in Norway and Denmark (less so in Sweden) suggests a tacit acceptance on the part of audiences of the generic qualities of the costume film over expectations of authenticity, which characterised the circulation of the heritage film a decade earlier. *I Am Dina* proves that the 'self-confident assumption of a banal commonality stimulates circulation in a way that has precisely the kind of denationalising effect that makes a genuinely transnational culture possible' (Hjort 2005: 211). The cast of European stars and the Scandinavian credentials of the project come together in a package in which the multi-national markers of identity overwrite former considerations of cultural authenticity and middlebrow appeal. In this respect, *I Am Dina*'s melodramatic flamboyance, sexual frankness and spectacular locations, including vistas of the Norwegian fjords, make for a new type of brash and confident popular European heritage film that casts off the duties of authenticity and tastefulness of earlier prestige films such as the Oscar-winning *Babette's Feast* and *Pelle Erobreren* (*Pelle the Conqueror*, Bille August, 1987).

This de-nationalising effect is crucial for the globe-trotting economy of heritage film production, which is often shaped by the need to tap into

European and local funds. Furthermore, transnational filmmaking tends to be encouraged by national film funds and policy makers, who see in American and European investors the potential to stimulate local production through the renting of local facilities and the employment of local crews. This can lead, however, to a hybrid aesthetic shaped by logistic choices. A journalist for the trade paper *Screendaily* notes that:

> At the heart of international co-productions lies an essential paradox for Europe. The various national incentive schemes and subsidies upon which they depend are designed to keep filmmaking crews and talents fully employed in their local countries. And yet, co-production treaties are meant to encourage cross-border collaborations ... This contradiction may help explain the tortured arrangements producers often find themselves entering into in order to satisfy the various national requirements to unlock their soft money enticements. (Neiiendam 2004)

To cite two high-profile examples, *Perfume: The Story of a Murderer* (Tom Tykwer, 2006) was shot in Barcelona in order to attract 20 per cent of the budget from Spain, whereas the Holland-set biopic *Girl with a Pearl Earring* was supported by a 25 per cent tax credit granted by Film Fund Luxembourg, to where the location shooting was moved accordingly (see Judell 2003). Economic-driven decisions increasingly shape production of the heritage film, whereas casting and script choices are made with the widest possible market in mind. Thus, the expectations raised by the best-selling source novels were matched by the casting of up-and-coming Ben Wishaw alongside Dustin Hoffman in *Perfume*, and of Scarlett Johansson alongside established heritage star Colin Firth in *Girl with a Pearl Earring*. These decisions helped the films secure international sales and resulted in counter-examples of imaginative (and commercially successful) English-language Europuddings. Drawing the emphasis away from culturally-specific elements such as language, both films stress production design and expressive cinematography towards the construction of hyper-detailed fictional worlds filtered through the point of view of their striking central characters (we shall return to *Girl with a Pearl Earring* in chapter 3).

Alongside this shift towards transnational productions and forms of storytelling, an important trend in the European heritage film is the return to traumatic national pasts. Some of the preferred subjects of the period film in the first decade of the twenty-first century have included the impact of ethnic and political repression against the backdrop of the defining conflicts of the twentieth century in Europe. In particular, the Spanish Civil War, the two World Wars, the Holocaust and the Troubles in Northern Ireland have been absorbed into a heritage culture that elicits forms of collective memory through the images and sounds of the recent past, which is fictionally re-enacted in the present tense. In the iconography of the twentieth-century retro film, it is not only period objects and fashions (the primary visual signifiers of period authenticity) that play a part, but also the audiovisual textures provided by photographs, popular music and newsreel footage that are central to what Lutz Koepnick calls a 'culture of post-memory' where so-called 'prosthetic techniques of recollection' have become the norm (2002: 49). In his discussion of the contemporary German heritage film, Koepnick observes the use of these visual techniques towards a recurrent fantasy of historical reconciliation in films that propose a German-Jewish consensus, such as the lesbian love story between a German housewife and a Jewish woman in the World War II drama *Aimée und Jaguar* (*Aimée and Jaguar*, Max Färberböck, 1999). The mediated evocation of place, character and atmosphere allows for a reinterpretation of wider historical events through changing (present) views of nation, gender and ethnicity.

It is possible to extend this search for consensus to a cycle of heritage films that seek to rehabilitate popular forms of memory against the backdrop of intensely politicised national histories. In this regard, there are aesthetic parallels between the *Ostalgie* phenomenon – popular German films, including *Sonnenallee* (*Sun Alley*, Leander Haussmann, 1999) and *Goodbye Lenin!* (Wolfgang Becker, 2003), that retrieve aspects of everyday life in the communist state of the German Democratic Republic – and Spanish retro-comedies like *Muertos de risa* (*Dying of Laughter*, Álex de la Iglesia, 1999) and *Torremolinos 73* (Pablo Berger, 2003), which explore popular subcultures that flourished during the transition from the military dictatorship of General Francisco Franco to democracy. Everyday life in totalitarian states gives an edge to these period films, which fulfil two functions: they mobilise media memories of specific political and cultural significance, and they tap into retro-fashions in comedies and coming-of-age dramas that target young audiences. It is the focus on the textures of memory, rather than direct political commentary, that constitutes the basis for what Svetlana Boym calls 'reflective nostalgia': a nostalgia whose affective power creates spaces for critical thinking (quoted in Enns 2007: 477).

Der Untergang (*Downfall*, Oliver Hirschbiegel, 2004) and *Das Leben der Anderen* (*The Lives of Others*, Florian Henckel von Donnersmarck, 2006) offer provocative examples of this trend by exploring political repression from the point of view of the perpetrators as well as the victims. *The Lives of Others* in particular uses darkened and de-saturated colours, widescreen compositions and meticulous sound design to present a claustrophobic space. Period detail becomes 'metaphorical hyperrealism', stressing melancholic images of life during the late and most repressive period of the GDR (Evelyn Finger quoted in Enns 2007: 490). *The Lives of Others* gives a new meaning to the heritage film by focusing on objects and spaces endowed with heightened emotional significance by the insidious threat of state surveillance. The film provides a balanced portrait of the psychological make-up and moral decisions of characters placed at both ends of the processes of political violence, largely adopting the point of view of a member of the Stasi (the state secret police), sympathetically played by Ulrich Mühe. This stance sparked controversy but functioned as a high-concept strategy in the mainstream, well supported by the film's humanistic discourse around the redemptive power of art and a tight character-driven structure.[4] These qualities made the film a favourite on the arthouse scene in 2007. Both *Downfall* and *The Lives of Others* were international hits that augmented the publicity exposure of the new cycle of political films, and provoked intense debates about the recuperation of traumatic heritages through engaging retro-fictions.

These films suggest a move away from the consensual national narratives that arose since World War II towards the reconfiguration of the myths of national identity in what could be called, borrowing from Mike Wayne, the 'anti-national' heritage film (2002: 59). Across other Western European countries, retro films that touch on the subject of political violence have signalled a renaissance of European political cinema, which takes the 1970s as a formative moment of national crisis and political radicalisation. For example, in *Buongiorno, notte* (*Good Morning, Night*, Marco Bellocchio, 2003), *Salvador* (*Puig Antich*) (Manuel Huerga, 2006), *Hunger* (Steve McQueen, 2008) and *Der Baader Meinhof Komplex* (*The Baader Meinhof Complex*, Uli Edel, 2008) the urgency of political drama inflects

Recreating the political past: surveillance and hyperrealism in *The Lives of Others*

period reconstruction. The films' focus on individuals who struggle against the state, and on state wars waged against the civil population who is transformed into the internal enemy, extends the significance of the role that collective memory plays in the erosion of myths of national identity. Mobilising a generic and intertextual appeal, each of these films evokes a long history of cinematic representations of the recent national past, be it Spanish films on the Francoist dictatorship, representations of the Red Army Faction in German cinema, works about political violence in Northern Ireland or films that deal with leftist terrorism in Italy. By fusing aspects of political docudrama, biopic and retro aesthetics, these films condense complex historical processes into individualised narratives that meditate on political violence even as they spectacularise it. If taken as part of a transnational cycle, this politically articulate heritage cinema represents a third phase after modernist historical drama and quality realism: a new wave of films that rebrand a controversial yet recognisable iconography of the nation for international circulation.

Likewise, genre and pastiche have provided new modes of memorialising the Holocaust as part of a European heritage, as comedy in *La vita è bella* (*Life is Beautiful*, Roberto Benigni, 1997), melodrama in *The Boy in the Striped Pyjamas* (Mark Herman, 2008) or indirectly as background to spectacular action/war dramas in *Zwartboek* (*Black Book*, Paul Verhoeven, 2006) and *Inglorious Basterds* (Quentin Tarantino, 2008). The latter two films in particular rework the World War II film as a multi-lingual, Euro-Hollywood spectacle that draws on a veritable map of crossed mythologies, tackling history as re-imagined through the memory of Hollywood and European genres. This complex map of national and international representations, facilitated by new frameworks of international cooperation, addresses national histories in a wider context marked as (geographically and generically) European.

Crossing over: the European heritage film in the era of global Hollywood

Prompted by the contact of European cinemas with global Hollywood the heritage film has entered a post-national phase. Side by side with the auteur and quality period films, European historical epics are designed to compete with Hollywood blockbusters in the international market. These multi-national films are often aligned with institutional initiatives of commemoration. *1492 Christophe Colomb* (*1492 Conquest of Paradise*, Ridley Scott, 1992) is an English-language, high-budget heritage film, only different from Hollywood blockbusters because of its French star (Gérard Depardieu) in the title role. The film was released to coincide with the quincentennial commemoration of Columbus' voyage to the Americas; commemoration that was tempered by criticism of the imperialist and racist language of the 'discovery' (see Graham & Sánchez 1995: 416). *Valmont* (Milos Forman, 1989), another English-language production made with French money, capitalised on the bicentennial of the French Revolution and on the Hollywood experience of its expatriate Czech director. Forman would later shoot another European project, *Los fantasmas de Goya* (*Goya's Ghosts,* 2006), an English-language biopic of the eponymous nineteeenth-century Spanish painter that was made in Spain with a cast including Javier Bardem, Stellan Skarsgård and Natalie Portman. These films follow in the steps of *Der Name der Rose* (*The Name of the Rose,* Jean-Jacques Annaud, 1986) and *The House of the Spirits* (Bille August, 1993): European super-productions shot in a neutral variety of 'international' English that seek to compete against the Hollywood blockbusters with literary and historical narratives enhanced by high-concept marketing. Martine Danan points out that these epics respond to the need for European cinemas to 'emulate the hegemonic Hollywood model while minimising national cultural specificities' (1996: 78). For Danan, this kind of cinema represents a postnational model of production:

> The 'postnational' mode of production erases most of the distinctive elements which have traditionally helped define the (maybe)

imaginary coherence of a national cinema against other cinematographic traditions or against Hollywood at a given point in time:
for example, an implict or explicit worldview, the construction of
national character and subjectivity, certain narrative discourses
and modes of address or intertextual references. (Ibid.)

The epic heritage film uses blockbuster marketing strategies (simultaneous release, market saturation and massive advertising campaigns) while
downplaying culturally specific elements and foregrounding generic ideas
about history. In *Goya's Ghosts* the relationship between the painter and
his mysterious model is the springboard for a story of intolerance and persecution that features the Spanish Inquisition and the Napoleonic inva-
sion. However, the efforts to put together a product that is attractive to
national and international audiences can result in an incongruous mode of
address. In *Goya's Ghosts* the distracting mixture of English and Spanish
dialogue on the soundtrack, the deployment of clichéd commonplaces
of Spanish history and a wooden performance from Spanish star Bardem
recall earlier 'Europudding' attempts at creating hybrid cultural products
and undermine the film's broad reflection on the mechanisms of political
repression.

Scholars of European cinema have noted the loss of a clear political
angle in favour of large-scale historical spectacle in transnational super-
productions. Costing roughly $100 million, the German-driven, American-
financed, *Enemy at the Gates* (Jean-Jacques Annaud, 2001), was one of the
most expensive European films of the 2000s. For Randall Halle, *Enemy at
the Gates* seeks to sell a specific episode of World War II (the defense of
Stalingrad from German attacks in the autumn of 1942) to a transnational
audience by turning it into a quasi-mythological tale that individualises the
forces of good and evil. As Halle notes, the film unfolds as 'a grand story
of battle and bravery told from a post-ideological perspective' (2002: 26),
thus suppressing any specific political alignment. The film addresses the
role of propaganda in armed conflict, yet focuses on the protracted confrontation between a Russian soldier (Jude Law) and a German sniper (Ed
Harris). In an effort to compete with Hollywood's monopoly on the World
War II film, *Enemy at the Gates* turns the Stalingrad front into the backdrop
for a showdown which, as Halle suggests, 'could have taken place in a
number of contexts: Bosnia, Beirut, Belfast or the "Wild West"' (2002:

27). In this respect, the film is an example of a post-national European cinema where the producer, as much as the auteur, is the creative motor. Luc Besson, head of EuropaCorp and director/producer of *The Messenger: The Story of Joan of Arc* (1999); Saul Zaentz, producer of *Amadeus* (Milos Forman, 1984), *The English Patient* (Anthony Minghella, 1996) and *Goya's Ghosts*; and Bernd Eichinger, producer of *The Name of the Rose* and *The House of the Spirits* as well as *Downfall* and *The Baader Meinhof Complex* have made their mark as key players in a European cinema with global ambitions. The epic heritage film represents the flip side of the festival-oriented, culturally specific cinema of auteurs traditionally associated with Europe.

Since the mid-1990s the European heritage film has entered a post-national phase in which aesthetic and industrial choices are often conditioned by the input of Hollywood studios with the ultimate goal of international market penetration. Halle notes that 'art cinema' has ceased to be an aesthetic category but remains one of the most significant routes through which European films enter North American markets (2002: 29). Unable to generate enough domestic revenue or access other national markets in an economically significant way, purely national productions are being displaced by multi-national co-productions and films financed through the intervention of the Hollywood majors. The ultimate goal is to break into the American market, which has traditionally been culturally adverse to foreign-language films.

The British heritage film is both a paradigmatic example and something of an exception in the landscape of post-national European cinema. Often regarded as closer to the United States than to Europe in terms of linguistic influence and industrial aspirations, the 'Europeanness' of British cinema is, to say the least, problematic (see Nowell-Smith 2004). The Conservative government's withdrawal of state support and of protectionist measures in the 1980s, and Britain's low-level commitment to the MEDIA programme and the Eurimages Fund in the 1990s (see Hill 2001; Christie 2004) further emphasise the importance of international revenue for the British cinema industry as well as its historical dependence on the American market. This economic context underpins the new directions taken by the debates on the heritage film. In his book *English Heritage, English Cinema: Costume Drama Since 1980*, Higson carries out a forceful re-contextualisation of the British heritage film, updating and re-mapping the debates onto the wider economic picture at the turn of the 2000s. Thus the cultural terms of the heritage critique mutate into an economic argument about the crossover film, a category that has become instrumental in relocating national cinemas in the global, Hollywood-dominated market. The medium-budget prestige film backed by British and American money of the 1980s (such as *A Passage to India*) that first evolved into the independently produced, art-house distributed hit (*Howards End*) has latterly become a product designed and/or supported by Hollywood studios (*Shakespeare in Love*, John Madden, 1998). This new kind of heritage film is designed to cater for the more specialised tastes of crucial niche markets, with the potential to reap the benefits of wide exposure. As Higson notes:

> Such films are driven by both the commercialism and the market imperative of the mainstream studio film and the cultural imperative and artistic values of the specialised film. Their budgets fall between the two stools too, and they frequently draw on funding sources associated with both sectors. And crucially, they are designed to be distributed on both the low-budget, often subsidised, art-house circuit and the mainstream, multiplex circuits, and to appeal to their different audiences. (2003: 91)

In the 1990s some medium-budget heritage films with crossover appeal became box office hits in the United States. With the support of the deep pockets and aggressive marketing practices of Disney-owned Miramax, *The English Patient* grossed $78 million in the US and *Shakespeare in Love* punched above the then 'magical' $100 million threshold. The international success of these heritage films demonstrated its potential beyond its middlebrow appeal. Furthermore, it was symptomatic of the expanding market for the art film in the late 1990s (see Pidduck 2004). Subsequent films (such as the 1990s cycle of Jane Austen adaptations) need to be understood not only in cultural terms, but also as part of production trends, that is, as 'products of a particular business strategy, a particular way of operating within the global film economy' (Higson 2004: 39). For the British film industry, this tends to mean stimulating the production of Hollywood films in the UK and creating British films with global appeal. This argument does not substantially alter the founding terms of the debate: indeed, quality, nostalgia and Englishness continue to be keywords throughout Higson's work. Nevertheless, the more the heritage film becomes a stylised time-capsule, designed with international audiences in mind and increasingly detached from the geopolitical lines of force in national cultures, the more the films resist one-way, national-oriented readings. The heritage film from the mid-1990s onwards should thus be considered instead as a fully-fledged international genre, based on iconographic conventions that can be creatively appropriated and re-encoded according to changing notions of realism, authenticity and ideological purpose in order to address diverse audiences.

Julika Griem and Eckart Voigts-Virchow claim that 'we need a conceptualisation not only of *national identity* but also of *genre* that no longer indirectly clings to the authentifying discourse of nostalgic heritage culture' (2002: 320; emphasis in original). The heritage film is not an industrially defined genre like the western, the romantic comedy or the horror thriller, yet it sits comfortably amongst them in an era of genre hybridisation, in which taste formations (the middlebrow and the quality film) can be matched to niche markets. The heritage film – alongside the chick flick, the date movie or the slasher-spoof – has turned into one among many 'new high-concept genres in which the audience defines the film' (Cubitt 2005: 344). As the heritage film seeks to spice up old classics through pastiche, genre borrowings and increasingly bold intertextual games (more often than not with an eye unabashedly set on the youth market, as in *Shakespeare in Love* or Baz Luhrmann's *Romeo + Juliet* (1996)), the critical focus has shifted away from national identity politics and issues of fidelity in the literary adaptation and towards what Voigts-Virchow describes as the new 'syncretic' character of heritage film culture since the mid-1990s. He argues that the 'regenrification' of the heritage film in the contexts of global production and consumption has become the new critical arena where the period drama is being repositioned (2004: 24–5). At the film industry's high end, the regenrification of the heritage film leads into the generic packaging of the literary adaptation as an integrated multimedia experience. Examples of this include the fantasy blockbuster franchises *The Lord of the Rings* (Peter Jackson, 2001–03), the cycle of *Harry Potter* films and the C. S. Lewis adaptations *The Chronicles of Narnia: The Lion, the Witch and the Wardrobe* (Andrew Adamson, 2005) and *The Chronicles of Narnia: Prince Caspian* (Andrew Adamson, 2008).

In the process, fast-developing new digital image technology is altering traditional representations of national identity. French blockbusters *Vidocq*

(Pitof, 2001) and *Le Pacte des loups* (*Brotherhood of the Wolf,* Christophe Gans, 2001) are driven by the attractions of fully-digitised visions of the past. In these films the landmarks of national identity (the urban space of nineteenth-century Paris in *Vidocq*; pre-revolutionary eighteenth-century France in *Brotherhood of the Wolf*) are reinvented as pure spectacle. As James F. Austin notes, in the digital era the French *patrimoine* or heritage film has entered a fully postmodern phase where the past has become 'quite intensely an aesthetic matter' (2004: 296). These films typically erase the dialectic between present and past in favour of immersing the viewer into a hyperreal past-in-the-present.

The consideration of heritage as a genre is a useful mode of addressing the way in which the heritage film is gradually changing into a 'post-' phenomenon: post-national, post-quality and post-modern. As films get made thanks to co-production schemes and European subsidies as well as the support of Hollywood global capital, they become increasingly difficult to pin down according to national or auteurist traits of style. This unprecedented level of internationalisation has re-shaped the British heritage film in particular. International filmmakers bring their position as outsiders to bear on their engagement with topics relating to British culture, as in the case of *Sense and Sensibility*, directed by Taiwanese Ang Lee, or *Elizabeth*, directed by Indian Shekhar Kapur. These exceptional films stand on the shoulders of what constitutes a tried and tested formula. In the late 1990s, a number of bland adaptations and biopics set in Europe, including *Immortal Beloved* (Bernard Rose, 1994), *Anna Karenina* (Bernard Rose, 1997), *Dangerous Beauty* (Marshall Herskovitz, 1998) and *Cousin Bette* (Des McAnuff, 1998) were made to capitalise on attractive locations and costumes, using American or (English-speaking) European stars. These run-of-the-mill period dramas secure international exposure through the global networks of distribution controlled by the Hollywood studios, which are, in turn, the property of multi-national conglomerates. The decentralised nature of the studios' commercial operations allows them to spread the risks across a variety of international investments. As Nick James notes, Hollywood's ubiquitousness can be read in two different ways: 'either as the perfect cover for the US industry's ruthless pursuit of global trade dominance, or as a genuine rapprochement that recognises and makes best use of the strengths of various national resources around the world' (2009: 21). Whether this should be considered a positive or negative development, the 'Euroamerican' costume film interestingly evokes a previous moment in American-European relations. In the 1950s the boom of co-operation with American studios (in the so-called Hollywood's 'runaway productions', shipped to European locations as a cost-cutting measure) as well as the rise of cosmopolitan European co-productions were the causes, in the words of Tim Bergfelder, for the nation to 'vanish' (at least momentarily) in the shadow of international cycles of popular comedies, adventure films and costume dramas (see 2000: 141–2).

The pressures of globalisation, however, continue to raise the ghost of the Europudding from time to time. Veteran film critic Jonathan Rosenbaum's stance on *The Luzhin Defence* (Marleen Gorris, 2000) is symptomatic of a widespread scepticism towards these international films. For Rosenbaum, the generic approach to the original source text (a little-known novel by Vladimir Nabokov) and the non-descript European locations make it 'virtually impossible to affix a national identity to any of the central characters, most of whom are Russian in the novel. Their names remain Russian, but their existential essences seem ruled to a ridiculous degree by the Europudding English they speak, which makes them come across as fugitives from nowhere' (2001). The flip side to the Europudding nowhere land is the simulacrum of European historical landscapes found in what James calls the 'Natopudding': Hollywood heritage films, often based on best-selling novels, which imagine a quasi-mythical European past reduced to a series of clearly coded cultural clichés: provincial France in *Chocolat* (Lasse Hallström, 2001), or the paradisiacal Greek islands in *Captain Corelli's Mandolin* (John Madden, 2001). These films mark a point of no return in the internationalisation and abstraction of the genre. Developed by the Disney subsidiary Miramax, they tried to replicate the success of European heritage films such as *Il Postino* and *Life is Beautiful*. *Chocolat*, an English-language fairytale narrative set in an indeterminate French small town has been called a 'formidable example of the transnational qualities of heritage culture' (Krewani 2004: 165). There was no French participation in the English-language *Chocolat*, but the casting of Juliette Binoche in the lead brings the necessary touch of connoted Frenchness to the proceedings. The emphasis on quaint crafts and feminine pleasures such as the making and consumption of chocolate carries the signs of Frenchness into a quasi-mythical, timeless land, where the European past can be conjured up as an exotic *Brigadoon*-like territory untainted by history or modernity.

However, the heritage genre has become flexible enough to accommodate works that mobilise the allure of the prestige film but are actually closer to the experimentation found in European art cinema traditions. Multi-national art films such as Sally Potter's *Orlando*, which will be discussed in chapter 3, *The English Patient*, *Le Violon rouge* (*The Red Violin*, François Girard, 1998) and *Sunshine* (István Szabó, 1999), as well as avant-garde forays into the literary adaptation and the biopic, most notably Raoul Ruiz's highly experimental *Le Temps retrouvé* (*Time Regained*, 1999) and *Klimt* (2006), use period reconstruction to incorporate meta-textual elements that stress a shifting sense of identity. They make non-linear conceptions of history accessible to diverse audiences but only *Orlando* and *The English Patient* were crossover hits. The widespread visibility of the 'Natopudding', in contrast to the more limited exposure of the experimental heritage film, begs the question of whether heritage film culture is able to cater for diversity when exploring history and memory, or whether it is merely symptomatic of the power of globalisation to force British and European film to retreat into the 'insipid mid-Atlanticism' denounced by Nowell-Smith (1997: 574).

The heritage film may have turned into a generic formula but it is one that, like all genres, admits imaginative aesthetic variation and is open to provocative forms of cultural hybridity that may bring diversity and renewal to national traditions. In the case of British cinema the focus on period spectacle and small-scale stories also reconnects it to Europe. Thus, when the landscapes of Russian Romanticism (in *Onegin*, Martha Fiennes, 1999) or the European artist's biopic (see the discussion of *Girl with a Pearl Earring* in chapter 3) receive the heritage treatment, the outcome is a dense visual aesthetic that uses familiar, clichéd images to stress character, longing and emotion. In Spain the quality horror/fantasy period film continues to evoke a traumatic national heritage: the Spanish Civil War of 1936–39 and the protracted fascist dictatorship that followed. The new horror films, however, are made also with international audiences in mind. Thus, the Gothic pastiche *Los otros* (*The Others*, Alejandro Amenábar, 2001) and the Spanish-Mexican co-productions by Guillermo del Toro *El espinazo del diablo* (*The Devil's Backbone,* 2001) and *El laberinto del fauno* (*Pan's Labyrinth*, 2006) use period settings and the child's gaze in ways that evoke 1970s allegorical films such as *El espíritu de la colmena* (*The Spirit of the Beehive*, Víctor Erice, 1973) but do not presuppose prior knowledge of Spanish political history. These films are both local and global, as they update the austere iconography and coded messages of a former cinema of political dissent into accessible and spectacular genre narratives that carry a national (anti-)heritage into post-national contexts.

The heritage film offers the perfect site for examining the internationalisation of national cinemas. The movement of funds as well as artistic and technical personnel is inevitable given the fragmented nature of national film industries in Europe. In this context, the heritage genre has constructed its own niche as part of an international popular film culture that exposes and occassionally interrogates received ideas about national identities. However, it also constitutes a belated phase in the rebranding of the national as a strategy for survival in the globalised market. In the final section of this chapter, we shall focus on one film, *Joyeux Noël*, to explore the two sides of this question further.

Joyeux Noël: popular memory, commemoration and the European heritage film

Joyeux Noël reflects the formation of a shared European memory that also embraces the particularities of national experience. A European co-production in which the characters speak English, French and German, Carion's film uses its World War I setting to refer to a common European past, albeit one of violent nationalistic conflict. *Joyeux Noël* is one of a number of contemporary co-productions about 'authentic multinational, multilanguage stories' (Kirschbaum 2005: 23), a category that also includes the World War II spy drama *Black Book*, and the student comedy *L'Auberge espagnole* (*Pot Luck*, Cédric Klapisch, 2002). These projects tap into supranational European funding to support national films that aspire to reach international audiences. *Joyeux Noël* offers a particularly interesting example of the potential and the limitations of the heritage film in this context of transnational co-operation and the formulation of a European identity.[5]

The film draws on accounts of unofficial wartime truces that occurred during World War I as the basis for its story about the December 1914 truce, during which French, British and German troops on the front line spontaneously decided to lay down their arms on Christmas Eve. In the film this temporary suspension of hostilities allows the different sides to bury their dead and engage in collective respite from war. The film project was led by French producer Christophe Rossignon and had a budget totalling €18 million ($23 million at the time) including Eurimages funds of €580,000. Production was a joint effort involving France's Nord-Ouest Productions, Germany's Senator Film Produktion, Romania's Media Pro Pictures, Belgium's Artemis Productions and the UK's The Bureau, along with support from the CNC and the *Filmforderungsanstalt* (FFA – the German Film Board), plus broadcasters from the countries involved. The trade paper *Variety* highlights the film as a prototypical example of a 'natural co-production' that avoids the 'Europudding curse' (Kirschbaum 2005: 23), since the multilingual screenplay employs English only in sections where the verisimilitude of characters and situations requires it. The project thus calls for multinational involvement, which, in turn, constitutes a 'natural' invitation to collaborate in economic terms (see Koehler 2005). The conditions of such collaboration can be usefully explained as an example of what Hjort calls 'epiphanic transnationalism':

> In epiphanic transnationalism the emphasis is on the cinematic articulation of those elements of deep national belonging that overlap with aspects of other national identities to produce something resembling deep transnational belonging. The term 'epiphanic' signals the extent to which this form of transnationalism depends on a process of disclosure that is also somewhat constitutive of the depicted commonalities. (2010: 16)

This practice is commonly found in small-scale projects put together by agents in different countries. As noted by Hjort, the Swedish-Danish co-production *Pelle the Conqueror*, a film that explores emigration from Sweden to Denmark in the nineteenth century, is an earlier example in which national identities are recognised in a transnational context. *Joyeux Noël* posits a more ambitious case of culturally motivated epiphanic transnationalism. The networks of collaboration involving funds and personnel from at least five countries not only obey the internal logic of the project, but also allow the film producers to bypass Hollywood studio funding. The French director and author of the screenplay, Christian Carion, defended this set-up as essential to the artistic integrity of the film, stressing the differences from the purely economic rationale of the Europudding. For Carion, 'the fact that everyone in the film speaks their own language makes it authentic' (quoted in Kirschbaum 2005: 23).[6] However, these terms of collaboration are also supported by other forms of unmarked transnationality (see Hjort 2010), such as the use of available locations (the film was partially shot in Bucharest's Media Pro Studios). Furthermore, the film circulated as a French production in the festival and non-European distribution circuits. *Joyeux Noël* was screened out of competition at the 2005 Cannes Film Festival, where it garnered positive reviews and, more importantly, was picked up for distribution in the US by the specialised studio branch Sony Pictures Classics. The film retained its French title in several of the territories where it was distributed (for example, the UK) and competed for a Golden Globe and an Academy Award as the official French entry in the Best Foreign Film category in 2006. Although a textbook example of a European production, *Joyeux Noël* can equally be regarded as the outcome of a national policy framework that promotes diversity, aiming at both cultural difference and commercial appeal in order to compete with Hollywood blockbusters (see Jäckel 2007). As such, it is a distinctive post-GATT film that illustrates the ways in which France continues to represent Europeanism while ultimately reasserting its own national interests (see Rivi 2007).

The film's dramatic structure mirrors its productions arrangements. *Joyeux Noël* opens with a montage of uncaptioned photographs and traditional paintings of idyllic country scenes. This montage incorporates the first bars of the central musical theme of the film, 'I'm Dreaming of Home'. This original composition by Philippe Rombi blends in with the traditional songs used elsewhere in the soundtrack (such as the carol 'Adeste Fideles/ Oh Come All Ye Faithful' and the Scottish traditional song 'Auld Lang Syne'). Such use of visual and aural pastiche sets a tone of diffused nostalgia for an idealised, pre-war past where focus is not on national specificity, but on the commonality of memory. The montage dissolves into a close-up of a map of the French/German border at the beginning of the twentieth century, an image that preludes a three-part sequence in which three children of similar ages standing at the front of empty, old-fashioned classrooms recite to the camera nationalistic poems against the enemy in French, English and German respectively. The allegorical mise-en-scène stresses education as a universal (and transhistorical) mechanism of ideological indoctrination that transforms children into national subjects. Throughout

Lessons in hatred: nationalist indoctrination in *Joyeux Noël*

the sequence, the camera glides forwards as the shot dissolves from one child to the next, accompanied by a sombre orchestral theme. This inexorable movement suggests the inevitable course of history leading towards armed conflict. With this self-conscious yet transparent statement, the film declares its intention to investigate a shared (popular) memory 'from below' as opposed to an official European history 'from above' founded on belligerent values of hatred towards the cultural Other that are transmitted from generation to generation.

The didactic opening sequence sets the tone through a narrative divided into three different perspectives on the conflict and three spaces that are, however, contiguous and similar: the French, Scottish and German trenches on the front line in the Nord-Pas-de-Calais region in Northern France. Segueing between the three main storylines, the film's first act endows the principal characters with poignant backstories. The first one follows Scottish Anglican pastor Palmer (Gary Lewis) who is accompanying two young brothers, Jonathan (Steven Robertson) and William (Robin Laing), recruited from a small town in the Highlands. When William is killed, Jonathan is left to cope with the loss, which he hides in his letters to their mother by signing them on his brother's behalf. In the second storyline, a German tenor (Benno Fürmann) and his fiancée, the Danish soprano Anna Sörensen (Diane Kruger) struggle to be reunited at the front. Their desire to be together at all costs clashes with the strict discipline of Horstmayer (Daniel Brühl), a German-Jewish lieutenant who mistrusts the singer as he believes him to be a less than capable soldier. In the third storyline, Audebert (Guillaume Canet), a French lieutenant who endeavours to endure being separated from the wife he has left behind in the occupied zone, and to cope with the absence of news about their newborn child, finds comfort in the friendship with his aide-de-camp, Ponchel (Dany Boon), a barber from the neighbouring region. These stories unfold largely within the constrained space of the trenches and the open no-man's-land that eventually becomes a terrain of death and mourning, but also of solidarity for all the troops. The plot interweaves the three storylines and levels the personal experiences of characters who are separated by opposed national allegiances, yet united by the common experience of loss and melancholy for the homes they left behind. 'Home' is rendered abstract and universal by the lyrics of the song 'I'm Dreaming of Home', yet palpable and specific by the tapestry of individual experiences and memories as well as the objects that symbolise them.

Joyeux Noël belongs to a cycle of French films committed to representing World War I from a pacifist stance. Films like Bertrand Tavernier's *La Vie et rien d'autre* (*Life and Nothing But,* 1989) and *Capitaine Conan* (*Captain Conan*, 1996), François Dupeyron's *La Chambre des officiers* (*The Officer's Ward*, 2001) and especially Jean-Pierre Jeunet's Warner Bros-financed *Un long dimanche de fiançailles* (*A Very Long Engagement,* 2004) cast a melancholic look at the conflict, focusing on the human cost while using the war as a backdrop for intimate stories. Laurent Véray calls *Joyeux Noël* a further example of the 'heritage-isation' (*la patrimonialisation*, in the French original) of World War I that responds to the anxieties caused by the difficulties surrounding the supra-national European project (the Cannes screening almost coincided with the negative outcome of the French referendum on the Treaty establishing a Constitution for Europe, held in May 2005) and the weakening of French-German relations (see Véray 2009). The humanistic rhetoric and accessible aesthetics of the film highlight the increasing synergy between mainstream popular culture and official discourses of public commemoration. For Thomas Elsaesser, this trend complements the heritage film with 'a more top-down version of re-instating the "national" as a valid and even vibrant incarnation of the idea of "Europe"' (2005: 72). Commemoration prescribes the 'increasing Europeanisation of what previously were national days of commemoration, as well as adding to the calendar anniversaries with a distinct European dimension' (ibid.) The tributes to the fallen in the two World Wars, the celebration of the D-Day landings and, especially, the tribute to the victims of the Holocaust have gradually become events that contribute to the fashioning of a common past through which 'Europe can affirm its core values of democracy and commitment to human rights, while condemning totalitarianism in all its forms' (2005: 73). Contemporary cinema is key to this commemorative culture and to the attendant formation of a 'common European "memory"' (2005: 74). However, as Elsaesser goes on to note, some of the high profile forays of mainstream film into these significant *lieux de mémoire* have been highly contested, whether as instances of American neo-imperialist appropriation (such as Steven Spielberg's *Schindler's List* (1993) and *Saving Private Ryan* (1998)), or as politically incorrect fictions emerging from European cinemas that are increasingly distancing themselves from modernist traditions (such as *Downfall*)).

Joyeux Noël's multi-perspective narrative and heritage 'authenticity' highlight this commemorative function. The political thrust of the film is conveyed, however, through the emotional 'truth' of its broad, humanistic message, and its selective focus on melodramatic story lines. Vast differences in experiences and background are neutralised by a homogenous mise-en-scène that joins the principal characters. Visual and aural cues connect all three spaces; using smooth continuity editing the film continuously cross-cuts between the three main storylines. For example, in the sequence after the opening credits, a single candle in the Scottish parish dissolves into a row of similar candles that line the stage of the Berlin Opera. A knock on the door of tenor Nikolaus Sprink's dressing room giving him two-minute notice of his stage entrance echoes a similar two-minute call that beckons Audebert to lead his men onto the battlefield. Likewise, the bloody outcome of the first clash between the French, Scottish and German troops is replaced by rapid cutting and reaction close-ups that stress the trauma of combat experienced by the men on all three sides. Audebert's first brush with death occurs when he finds himself lying next to the inert head and open eyes of a young soldier in his regiment. This encounter matches a similar shot/reverse-shot structure that joins the Scottish soldier Jonathan to the dead body of his brother, which he will be forced to leave behind.

In contrast with the intellectualised approach to war in films such as *Paths of Glory* (Stanley Kubrick, 1957), the unsparing *Idi i smotri* (*Come and See*, Elem Klimov, 1985) or the corporeal realism of the spectacular *Saving Private Ryan*, *Joyeux Noël* retreats into a measured classicism that focuses on character and highlights the emotive qualities of the close-up. The attention to faces (reaction shots abound throughout the film) disperses the call for political action into multiple sites of identification and personal experience, and avoids confronting the audience with the physical effects of violence. This sanitised approach to war was received with scepticism. The French film journal *Positif* issued a scathing review of *Joyeux Noël* that ridiculed the depiction of an 'immaculate war front' (Thabourey 2005: 59). In a separate piece in *Positif*, Roland Duval charged the film with 'shamelessly romanticising the hell of the trenches ... by drowning the bloodshed left by an unspeakable carnage in streams of retro-compassion' (2007: 140; author's translation). Indeed, we may wonder about the dangers of recasting the artistic and political heritage of European cinema exemplified by films such as *La Grande illusion* (Jean Renoir, 1937), which serves as distant and illustrious model for *Joyeux Noël*, into the programmatic remit of an official culture of commemoration. *Joyeux Noël*'s celebration of a pan-European past solely through the symbols of white, Christian Europe, as represented by the main Western colonial powers, is especially problematic in a film whose politically neutral stance and humanist universalism can be regarded as simplistic and highly ideological.

The above reading would reinforce, however, a hegemonic narrative of history that the film carefully alludes to in its opening schoolroom sequence and then disputes with its account of fraternisation during wartime. Instead, we should take a closer look at the confined heritage space of the film as a *performative* space for the enactment of an epiphanic transnationalism; that is, a fictional space with the potential for the 'cinematic articulation of those elements of deep national belonging that overlap with aspects of other national identities to produce something resembling deep transnational belonging' (Hjort 2010: 16). In this respect, the message of unity in diversity, which invests the 'Europeanness' of the film with political value, needs to be examined alongside the construction of a communicative space mediated through linguistic and iconographic clichés. Bagpipes, champagne and opera work as discursive shortcuts to national identities, while colloquial language draws attention to deep-seated prejudices. Signs on the trenches point towards 'Rosbif land' (on the French side) and 'Froggy land' (on the British side), thereby extending, in a humorous fashion, the predictable use of pejorative nicknames used to refer to the German enemy ('Jerries', 'Krauts', 'Boches'). These reductive images of nation, self-consciously deployed by the multi-national perspective upheld by *Joyeux Noël* suggest ways in which the heritage film works in terms of, to borrow from Elsaesser, 'impersoNation' or 'self-othering': presenting the Self (one's own national culture) through the look of the Other, including 'self-conscious, ironic or self-mocking display of clichés and prejudices' (2005: 61). The mapping of co-production arrangements onto narrative themes in *Joyeux Noël* points out the ways that cultural misreadings, or 'impersoNations', enable the national to travel across borders. Characters and interactions are reduced to iconographic and cultural clichés about Scotland, Germany and France that are broadly recognisable to international audiences. At the same time, the theme of fraternisation during wartime mobilises this clichéd performance of nation to highlight the paradoxical nature of nationalistic conflict and a shared traumatic history.

In the heritage film, history is visualised through space. Elements of mise-en-scène and sound design are shared by different sections of the front, constructing bonds of common experience between enemies. The alarm clock set at ten in the morning by Ponchel as a reminder of his everyday life during peace time helps Horstmayer to mark time. The cat that wanders freely between the trenches responds to different names (Felix for the German soldier Jörg; Néstor for Ponchel). This use of detail to highlight the proximity between enemies reaches its climax on Christmas Eve, when music draws the different characters – and narrative strands – together. When the songs played by the bagpipers in the Scottish trenches are heard across French and German lines, Sprink responds with his own singing of the carols 'Stille Nacht/Silent Night' and 'Adeste Fideles/Oh Come All Ye Faithful', and he is then joined by the Scottish pipers. This prompts Sprink to abandon the 'safe' space of the trenches and venture out into the no-man's-land that separates the different national troops as he carries on singing, holding up a small Christmas tree as a symbol of peace. Traditional music spontaneously creates a common space for the temporary suspension of hostilities, where first the lieutenants, and then the soldiers from both sides quickly follow. The Christmas carol, instantly familiar to the Scottish, the French and the German armies, allows the soldiers to recognise each other's humanity and form bonds through the exchange of objects: pictures of wives and girlfriends, chocolate, coffee cups and bottles of champagne become tokens of fraternisation that overcome language barriers. National differences are put aside as all three groups bury their dead and play football together.

The film is careful to endow religious symbols with a wider, secular resonance. Anna's singing of a religious hymn (originally composed by Rombi for the film) during the celebration of a Christmas Eve Mass is given a special weight. The focus on the singer's ability to *move* all men, regardless of nationality, reinforces the notion of art as a secular and more inclusive space than the liturgy delivered in Latin (another marker of neutrality) by Palmer. Likewise, the Scottish officer's remark, 'burying the dead the day that Christ was born – it makes sense', shifts the religious significance of Christmas towards a more general message about basic respect for human life. The opposition between religion as a doctrine amenable to nationalistic propaganda and religion as an expression of grassroots solidarity is highlighted in a sequence that cross-cuts between Palmer, who is seen tending to the wounded, and the homily delivered by a bishop to a fresh contingent of British soldiers. The bishop's call to arms against the German enemy ('you are the very defenders of civilisation itself, the forces of good against the forces of evil') is an example of the use of factual material (it is based on an actual homily delivered at Westminster Abbey in 1914) to reinforce the significance of the film's message of remembrance.[7] The incendiary tone of the bishop's address ('you must kill the Germans ... so it won't have to be done again') not only links both World Wars within the same cycle of nationalistic violence but also, in 2005, resonated with special force against the backdrop of ongoing public debate about Christian and Islamic fundamentalism in a Europe profoundly divided around the topic of American and European intervention in Iraq.

Creating a space for fraternisation: *Joyeux Noël*

The critique of power is, however, largely relegated to the background, as personal counter-histories take centre-stage. Audebert loses his wallet containing the cherished picture of his wife on the battlefield, but the wallet is returned to him by Horstmayer who, in turn, reveals in fluent French that he is married to a French woman. Such moments of personal disclosure overthrow national allegiances, emphasising the generational nature of political conflict. In this regard, the belated revelation that the general in command who pressures the young Audebert to accept military discipline is none other than Audebert's own father, recasts the young man's impassioned protest ('you don't live the same war as we do!') into the territory of family melodrama. This recourse to melodramatic emotion may foreclose the reach of the political critique but it also mobilises other modes of resistance to the glorification of war. Thus, for example, the intense and traumatic attachment of Jonathan to his brother William recalls the kind of imagery contained within the anti-war poetry of Wilfred Owen and Siegfried Sassoon, as well as the testimonies of shell-shocked soldiers associated with World War I. A close-up of Anna and Spink, the heterosexual couple sleeping in the trenches under the same blanket, cuts via a graphic match to a close-up of Jonathan lying close to the dead body of his brother. The unlikely scenario of an opera singer joining her beloved on the front line (a romantic subplot designed to enhance the commercial appeal of the film) does not detract from the fact that the 'tears of melodrama', the moving effect caused by recognition that comes too late (Neale 1986: 8), are reserved to scenes that depict homoerotic bonds between men. In particular, Ponchel's death (as the mistaken victim of Jonathan's rage against the Germans) notably feminises the *aide-de-camp*, who dies in Audebert's arms after muttering the words 'you have a son'. This retrenchment into the personal and the intimate stresses time and again the importance of communicating cultural content in an accessible language that reaches across national borders.

Finally, the film's move towards an international culture of commemoration and a pan-European discourse on difference and tolerance is achieved via the heterogeneity of the national in a post-national era (see Danan 1996). In a strategic move to de-centre national identity, the film's dramatic structure highlights alternative identities within nations. Ponchel's local Northern accent draws on the comic persona of Dany Boon, who hails from the Nord-Pas-de-Calais region. The 'difference' of the Scottish contingent is exoticised through the strong markers of Scottishness (accented English and bagpipes) but it also plays as an oppositional element within a national hierarchy dominated by the English. Most poignantly, Horstmayer's Jewish identity works as a tragic reminder of the destiny of minority ethnic groups in nationalistic conflict. In the closing sequence, Horstmayer and his men are deported to the Russian front (the true deadly off-screen space of war) in closed train wagons. The long shot of the anonymous, sealed train carriages that take the German soldiers to slaughter constitutes a powerful visual reminder of the trains that would carry the Jewish population to extermination camps less than thirty years later. This charged gesture towards the retrospective historical knowledge of the audience facilitates a direct transhistorical reflection on the cyclical processes of destruction and violence, and enhances the pacifist message of the film and its commemorative function.

Joyeux Noël can be seen as part of a post-1989 reflection on a shared heritage of conflict that, as Luisa Rivi has put it, 'includes, but does not replace, national industries, local contributions, and cultural and regional specificities' in order to '"invent" different Europes for a national, supranational, and global audience' (2007: 65). Unlike more radical low-budget co-productions such as *Land and Freedom* (*Tierra y Libertad*, Ken Loach, 1995), a film about the experience of members of the International Brigades fighting in the Spanish Civil War, *Joyeux Noël* self-consciously combines high production values and a classicist narrative. However, language and performance reinforce the film's heritage authenticity against Hollywood's language-blind approach to national stereotyping seen in World War II films such as *Captain Corelli's Mandolin*. Actors' accents and linguistic inflections largely match their characters' national identities, and they all speak their first language (even if English and French are allotted a larger portion of screen time). An astute casting of young leads with international appeal, which includes Guillaume Canet, Diane Kruger and Daniel Brühl (who brings intertextual associations with other films with political content such as *Good Bye Lenin!*) alongside Scottish character actor Gary Lewis and French comedy star Boon, maximises the presence of regional, national and multilingual stars in support of the film's Europeanist message.

Elsaesser remarks that European values of solidarity, pacifism and the commemoration of the past have proved 'less inspirational' than the universalising agenda of the Hollywood film, and have certainly not translated into the same kind of recognition for European cinema (2005: 60). European heritage films like *Joyeux Noël* try to fill that gap with a narrative model for contemporary European cinema that is both economically viable and ideologically potent. Rather than settling for a culturally blurred 'Europudding' aesthetic, the film maximises its appeal across national borders by multiplying the markers of national difference at the level of storytelling, language and performance. As Rivi notes, the 'national' has not been weakened by the push to construct a European identity in film:

> It is precisely the nationally and locally specific traits that are responsible for the make-up and success of European cinema. Co-productions do not create a European cinema because they eliminate borders and employ identical narrative formulas. They contribute rather to the proliferation of European cinema if they preserve and acknowledge the marked differences of 'national', regional or local cinemas in Europe. (2007: 48)

Joyeux Noël draws on stereotypes for the recreation of a shared past that is not oblivious to sub-national difference and nationalistic conflict, elements that the film seeks to integrate as part of a wider supra-national shared memory within the remit of official commemorative culture. Unsurprisingly, the film's 'Europeanising' stance stays well within the limits of consensual representation. However, this does not invalidate *Joyeux Noël* as a film seeking to produce a viable model for a popular European cinema that builds on the traits of the quality heritage film (such as production values and strong performances) and whose investment in authenticity is tied to characterisation and emotion. The retrospective construction of national difference passes through the deployment of familiar images and myths, which constitute a shared idiom with the potential to cross over borders. This defines the strengths and limitations of the European heritage film.

Notes

1   This was the title of the keynote address delivered by Galt at the Popular Italian Cinema conference held at King's College London, 28 May 2009.

2   Set up originally in 1987 by the European Community to support the audiovisual sector in Europe and protect minority languages, the diverse phases of the MEDIA programme have covered initiatives related to professional training, production, distribution, dubbing and subtitling of audiovisual projects (see Jäckel 2003: 68).

3   For example, with a contribution of DKr 16.4 million, Danish film companies are said to have received approximately €8m (DKr 60 million) from Eurimages during the 1990s (Brandstrup & Redvall 2005: 147). Britain notoriously withdrew from the fund in 1996 after only four years of membership (see Jäckel 2003: 77). Complaints from Italy and Holland, who have also threatened to withdraw from the scheme, have prompted further discussions about reforms in the system of contributions (see Macnab 2009).

4   In a cover article published in *Sight and Sound* on the occasion of the film's release in Britain, Anna Funder strongly criticises it as a fable that 'falsifies a fundamental truth about the regime in order to make a more uplifting entertainment' (2007: 16).

5   This section is indebted to the research conducted by Mariana Liz on 'European Identity in European Cinemas', PhD thesis in progress at the department of Film Studies, King's College London.

6   However, it must not be forgotten that the practice of dubbing prevalent in various European states (including France, Germany and Spain) would undermine the film's international mode of address upon its release in mainstream cinemas.

7   Christian Carion, DVD commentary. *Joyeux Noël*. DVD. Sony Pictures Home Entertainment, 2007.

3   NARRATIVE AESTHETICS AND GENDERED HISTORIES:
      RENEWING THE HERITAGE FILM

As we have seen in previous chapters, the heritage film debate of the 1990s singled out a return to former models of quality cinema and the emergence of a distinctive iconography of the national past. This debate ran parallel to the renewed popularity of the period film in Europe as a flexible category situated between popular national cinemas and the international art film. The contemporary heritage film has evolved beyond consensual visions of the past and into a multi-faceted genre that demands a revision of the original debates. This chapter explores alternative and revised critical responses to the heritage film focusing on the links between gender and genre; the critique of gender politics informs the central analysis of *Girl with a Pearl Earring*. This European co-production (shot partly in Luxembourg by a British director, with a British and North American cast) is significant in terms of the global projection of the British heritage film and its engagement with a European cultural past. Drawing on the conventions of both the romantic drama and the film biopic, *Girl with a Pearl Earring* offers productive terrain for the study of the revisionist histories and generic viewing pleasures afforded by the contemporary heritage film.

Women's histories and feminist politics

In 1993, when Andrew Higson's influential essay on heritage film was first published, a period drama set in nineteenth-century New Zealand carried off the prestigious Palme d'Or at the Cannes Film Festival. Jane Campion's *The Piano* was a landmark film for diverse reasons. It set a precedent by successfully crossing over from the art-cinema circuit to the multiplex. Made on a modest budget of $8 million, the film was picked up by Miramax and built into a critical and box office success (it would gross over $116 million across the world) (see Pidduck 2004: 9). *The Piano* engages with the British heritage film from a post-colonial position, proposing a bold reinvention of the Victorian imaginary. Prior to *The Piano*, however, another auteur period film had subverted the distinctive iconography of Englishness at the centre of the heritage film. Sally Potter's *Orlando*, an experimental adaptation partially shot in Russia and Uzbekistan and made with British, Russian, French, Italian and Dutch participation, takes its inspiration from the modernist literary tradition (the film adapts a novel by Virginia Woolf) to enact a postmodern dismantling of the classicist realism of the costume film and of the tropes of British heritage cinema. Both films emerge as towering examples of the crossover success of independent feminist filmmaking in the 1990s. While drawing on experimental and avant-garde practices, these period films benefit from the market niches opened by the success of 1980s heritage cinema. Thus they bring to the fore the possibilities of the genre for aesthetic creativity and political comment.

In a key study of the forms and politics of the contemporary costume film, Julianne Pidduck addresses these innovative art films as part of a

> quintessentially 'feminine' genre characterised by limited character mobility or physical, social and corporeal constraint ... The characteristic slowness and digression of these films ... contrasts with a pervasive trajectory of female becoming against fraught backgrounds of class and colonial struggle. (2004: 16)

While engaging with the terms of the heritage film debate, Pidduck proposes a feminist critique that reads the contemporary costume film differently, emphasising the creative juxtapositions between 'presentist' sensibility and past iconography, as well as the potential room (and limitations) for a gender critique that intersects with discourses of nation, race and class. *Orlando* and *The Piano* emerge as key films in this respect, as they take to task patriarchal constructions of culture and nation to reflect on an alternative heritage.

The plot of *The Piano* follows Ada (Holly Hunter), a Scottish woman who refuses to speak, as she enters an arranged marriage with Stewart (Sam

Neill), a settler in New Zealand, where she arrives accompanied by her young daughter Flora (Anna Paquin) and her piano. When Stewart forces her to leave the piano on the beach, his neighbour Baines (Harvey Keitel) gets hold of it and promises to return it to Ada in exchange for piano lessons. Although initially wary of his approaches Ada soon starts a passionate affair with Baines. Stewart's attempts to confine his wife and change her feelings turn into anger when Flora, out of jealousy, betrays her mother and shows him a love message inscribed on a piano key and addressed to Baines. In a bout of fury Stewart cuts off one of Ada's fingers and locks her up. When he finally lets her go Ada confronts the real choice of leaving her piano behind for a new life with Baines and Flora.

Even more than its bold narrative and adult content, *The Piano*'s strikingly modern mise-en-scène marks a departure from the prominence of the literary word associated with the British heritage film. Some of the film's most disturbing elements include a love story stemming out of blackmail, feminine mutilation, an ambiguous sexual triangle and a fraught yet intense mother/daughter relationship. The central promotional image, which shows a woman in full black Victorian attire and a young girl stranded on an open beach alongside a piano, became an iconic symbol of 1990s art cinema. This image encapsulates the notion of looking anew at a familiar iconography, reflecting the film's reading of tropes of Victorian culture from a point of view that is distinctively feminist and postmodern.

As Stella Bruzzi (1997) notes, *The Piano* provides an innovative 'sexual model' in women's filmmaking through the use of costume. Focusing on the discursive function of clothes, Bruzzi points out the difference between a liberal model of retrieving the past in heritage films such as *Sense and Sensibility*, which look *through* clothes as self-effacing signifiers of historical and literary authenticity, and a sexual model that looks *at* clothes, privileging sexuality and eroticism. The popular costume film provides examples of the latter, where clothes bring out an element of fantasy and escapist spectacle while raising attention on conflicting discourses on femininity (for example, in the 1940s Gainsborough cycle of period melodramas; more on this later). When adapted by women filmmakers, the sexual model 'foregrounds the emotional and repressed aspects of past women's lives and maps out an alternative but equally gendered territory that centres on the erotic' (Bruzzi 1997: 36). Ada's Victorian attire and her almost compulsive piano-playing construct a strong central female character out of elements traditionally associated with demure femininity. Both cumbersome and protective, her bonnets, voluminous crinoline skirts and petticoats and tight bodices hamper her movements in the hostile environment of the bush, but also formulate a language of secretiveness and revelation. They protect her from her husband's assaults and enable her to establish an erotic relationship with Baines, whereas the male characters are also defined by their adoption of or resistance to Victorian formal attire. Stewart's tall hats and waistcoats come across as uncomfortable and incongruous, whereas Baines' hybrid appearance (he dresses like the settlers, but sports Maori tattoos) connotes his in-between status and empathy with the Maori community (he evokes the trope of the European settler 'gone native').

Baines' characterisation highlights the problematic colonial trope in the film (as noted by Pihama (2000) and Pidduck (2004), among others). He represents an idealised appropriation of Maori identity as sensual, primitive and close to nature, whilst the actual Maori characters (and performers) are relegated to the background of the love triangle between the white settlers. However, the presence of the Maori community allows for moments of pointed criticism of the brutality of the underlying mythical structures as well as the actual social relations imported by the colonisers. In a sequence in which Ada plays along with the part of dutiful wife and mother by attending a school play based on the traditional tale of

A sensuous language: *The Piano*

Bluebeard, the play is brought to a halt by Maori members of the audience, who react with rage against the illusion of beheaded women on stage. The Maori may appear unsophisticated spectators duped by a fiction, yet the narrative invites us to read their gesture as one of symbolic revolt against the real violence that will be inflicted on Ada later in the film.

By interweaving feminist and post-colonial themes *The Piano* reads the popular imaginary of the Victorian novel through the ambiguity of art cinema. Based on an original script by Campion, reviewers and critics have noted the film's links to a body of nineteenth-century literature, from Gothic stories to Gustave Flaubert's classic *Madame Bovary* (see Gelder 1999). However, *The Piano* owes its status as cult film for women (see Klinger 2006) to the lasting impact of its iconography. The double ending, in which Ada both dies by drowning and is reborn again to a new life with the man of her choice, juxtaposes the kind of narrative closure associated to fairytales with the disturbing, yet aesthetically striking image of Ada's body shrouded in her ballooning skirts and buried at the bottom of the sea alongside her beloved piano. The piano thus remains an unresolved motif, both an instrument of personal expression, and a symbol of the weight of cultural inheritance on the bodies of women as well as of the limited agency granted to them by tradition.

The Piano's visual imagination demonstrates the potential of the costume film to open up established cultural themes to new frameworks of interpretation. Its motifs also crossed over to the mainstream, influencing other popular heritage films and television serials, for example the neo-Gothic *The Governess* (Sandra Goldbacher, 1998) or the unnerving story of domestic abuse in *The Tenant of Wildfell Hall* (BBC/CBC/WGBH, 1996) (see Caughie 2000). The sexual model noted by Bruzzi suggests a form of reclaiming the past that unearths hidden aspects of feminine identity but which also complicates feminist narratives with representations of female sexuality that test the limits of liberal feminism. This model can be mapped most clearly onto the 1990s, as opposed to the 1970s 'liberal' model of feminist narratives that concentrates on finding 'a political and ideological affinity between the struggles of women in the present and figures from the past' (Bruzzi 1996: 233). Narratives of oppression and self-fulfilment help to establish parallels between the political struggles of second- and first-wave feminism in films such as *My Brilliant Career* (Gillian Armstrong, 1979). In contrast, *The Piano* notoriously dwells on scenarios of sexual objectification and abuse that expose not only the mechanisms of patriarchal oppression but also the taboos of feminine desire. *The Piano*'s evocative images function as 'site of lingering affective power and uncertain meaning' (Klinger 2006: 21), and juxtapose a complex feminist consciousness with a re-reading of women's histories.

Sally Potter's *Orlando* takes the reflection on the different ages of feminism one step further. *Orlando* unfolds as a poetic journey through five hundred years of English history through the eyes and actions of a character who changes sex, from man to woman. Based on a modernist novel by Virginia Woolf (*Orlando: A Biography*, 1928) the film draws on the conventions of the period film as well as on Potter's own experimental film practice (in short films such as *Thriller* (1979) and *The Gold Diggers* (1983)). *Orlando* transforms the orderly landscapes of the heritage film into a gender-bender hall of mirrors, divided into self-enclosed historical vignettes. Each section is preceded by an intertitle, forming a sequence that covers Orlando's life journey, both as a man and as a woman, from '1600 Death' to 'Birth' (undated, but clearly located in the 1990s), passing through '1610 Love', '1650 Poetry', '1700 Politics', '1750 Society' and '1800 Sex'. By rigorously fragmenting space and time into a series of 'tableaux' or 'movements' (see Pidduck 2004: 105) the film comes across as a multi-faceted portrait of the central character, mediated by Orlando's enigmatic mode of address.

Orlando's deadpan look at the camera punctuates the film with humorous moments of distanciation, tending a bridge between the literary modernism of Woolf's novel and the pleasures of the heritage spectacle. This device transforms Orlando (Tilda Swinton) into a hero/ine who does not command narrative progression (the character does not evolve or mature in a conventional, 'psychological' way) but wanders through historical scenarios, providing a playful point of identification for the spectator. Orlando's simple quest for 'company', symbolic of the inclusive (and pansexual) 'humanness' defended by the film, encounters history as a series of gendered power structures in which s/he finds him/herself involved, and, both as a woman and a man, entrapped. However, only as a woman can Orlando articulate the critical view necessary to extricate herself from her historical 'destiny'. Herein lies the film's fundamental re-reading of the novel: as Roberta Garrett points out, to Woolf's gender indeterminacy Potter opposes 'strategic' female subjectivity (1995: 94). Constrained by masculine, linear history, Orlando's look/mode of address is deliberately

Knowing glances: Tilda Swinton in *Orlando*

female and feminist, and the experience of time represented in the film, cyclical and presentist (see Pidduck 2004: 108–9).

Orlando's ironic glances to the camera introduce a contemporary consciousness; they alternate with conventional close-ups registering her continuous bewilderment as a character of/beyond its time. The segmented narrative constructs Orlando as both an active participant and spectator of his/her own story, able to adopt a myriad of roles and gender identities organised around certain spatial constants. Places and objects accentuate repetition in the midst of vertiginous change, for instance the oak tree that bookends the narrative and thus provides a durable image of 'eternal England', or the house bestowed to Orlando by Elizabeth I. Likewise, certain gestures are echoed through the eras (loyalty and servitude are signified by the bowl of water presented to Queen Elizabeth by the young nobleman Orlando, and then by the offering of a bowl of water to a male lover by Orlando, the Victorian woman) whereas other gestures accrue an ironic resonance. In the '1610 Love' segment, Orlando declares his love to Sasha, the Muscovite ambassador's daughter, with absolute conviction: 'you are mine because I adore you'. Later, Orlando responds with amazement 'on what grounds?' to an identical declaration by Archduke Harry, which closes the '1750 Society' segment. These ironic repetitions undermine the romance narrative that defines the heroine's trajectory in the costume film.

The different tableaux compose a fragmentary history of imperial England through the ages, in which Orlando, as the opening voice-over states, seems 'destined to have his portrait on the wall and his name in the History books'. However, the film's progression articulates instead a series of subversive variations, leading to Orlando's progressive extrication from such destiny. Orlando's accumulated knowledge constitutes an alternative memory at odds with the master narrative of History but one which acknowledges its own limited viewpoint. In Potter's *Orlando*, as in Woolf's, 'costumes and selves are easily, fluidly, interchangeable' (Gilbert & Gubar 1989: 344). However, the feminist subject drawn by the film, although always in transition and movement, is solidly anchored by the body of the actress playing the part. Swinton cemented her early star persona as muse of the British avant-garde, especially through her work with Derek Jarman. Yet her face, often in close-up, also becomes an iconic site of identification that is white, bourgeois and English.

Orlando's brief experience of the colonial enterprise in the '1750 Politics' segment reflects on the feminist heritage film's problematic engagement with colonial histories. Refusing to participate as an active agent of repression in order to defend the economic interests of England in the 'East' (located in Khiva, Uzbekistan) Orlando reaches an impasse. He collapses to awake as a woman and returns to her countryside estate. As Pidduck points out, 'crisis of empire becomes crisis in masculinity, a timely disengagement from distasteful matters of statesmanship and empire' (2004: 112). As a woman in 1750, however, Orlando finds herself cornered into a no-win situation, in which the alternatives are legal death and dispossession, or a marriage of convenience in order to keep her property. The romantic space of the garden, a recurring motif in the heritage film, prompts a marriage proposition that provokes a new 'escape'. Orlando vertiginously propels herself through a garden maze that lands her into the nineteenth century. Interruption, like repetition, challenges the teleological view of history. Although chronological evolution is maintained as a staple convention of the biography genre, no phase ever reaches completion, no transition is smooth. Rather, each historical episode poses, literally and metaphorically, a crude awakening for Orlando (her entry into the twentieth century takes place directly into the battlefield of World War I).

Orlando's implausible yet exhilarating escapes from intolerable historical conjunctions mirror the film's own idiosyncratic rewriting of the heritage film in terms of the anachronistic (because utopian) gestures of feminist revision. Acknowledging at all times the fantasy quality of the past, *Orlando* is an ever-shifting artefact that compresses past, present and future. Potter's feminist film relies on the kaleidoscopic portrait that emerges out of the fragments, the dead-ends, the non-resolved questions and other rejects from history. The film finishes with a neat rounding gesture, having Orlando sit against the same oak where he is first 'unveiled' as a young man in the 1600s. However, she has come a long away and so has the film. The end of the film is nothing but a new beginning: the sparer, urban mise-en-scène offers a perfect background for a mobile, motorised Orlando (and her daughter) transformed into another casual visitor in her formerly-owned estate – now, ironically, in the hands of the heritage industry (see Ouditt 1999). Whereas the final shot of Orlando sitting under the oak comes loaded with the meanings of the past, the trembling framing of the camcorder operated by Orlando's young daughter signifies a mode of vision projected into the future. The last frame loses the background, narrowing down to a close-up of Orlando, staring back to the present, under the wing of the androgynous angel that closes the divide of gender and, by extension, the divide between past and present marked by linear historical time. *Orlando* redefines the British heritage film as a utopian text equally invested in masculinity and femininity, equally concerned with the future and with the past.

Whilst vastly different in tone and scope, *The Piano* and *Orlando* both enrich and challenge the dominant terms of the debate around the heritage film. Their aesthetic undoes nostalgic national myths and bring to the fore a critical sense of historicity. Whereas period drama is often considered a 'feminine' genre (one where women viewers could feel 'at home' whether in melodramas, romances or comedies of manners) *Orlando* and *The Piano* re-formulate women's history as counter-histories of uneasiness and resistance.[1] The traditional heroine of costume drama was either confined to the taming spaces of gardens and drawing rooms or, on the contrary, enjoyed fantasy scenarios of adventure and social mobility. Conversely, *Orlando* and *The Piano* dwell on the effort and costs involved in the attainment of such mobility (see Pidduck 2004) and, in the process, reinvest the genre with a sense of urgency. By bringing the generic conventions of the period film to a new level of formal postmodernism, women's filmmaking puts gender high on the agenda of the heritage film debate.

Post-heritage aesthetics and pastiche

Writing soon after the film's release, Claire Monk discussed *The Piano* as part of an emerging strand of period/literary films 'with a deep self-consciousness about how the past is represented' (2001: 7). This cycle, in which Monk included *Orlando* as well as the more conventional biopic *Carrington* (Christopher Hampton, 1995), exhibits 'an overt concern with sexuality and gender, particularly non-dominant gender and sexual identities: feminine, non-masculine, mutable, androgynous, ambiguous' (ibid.). For Monk, these are *post-heritage* films that continue to develop the potential of the heritage film. In particular, they carry out a reflection on gender politics initiated by the Merchant Ivory films of the 1980s. Monk suggests that the archetypal heritage films *A Room with a View* and *Maurice* present journeys of personal and sexual discovery that offer 'plentiful postmodern pleasures: of the performative, of self-referentiality and irony' (2001: 9). Her different appraisal of the heritage film points to areas of meaning excluded by the ideological critique of nostalgia, notably 'the consistent emphasis throughout *A Room with a View* on the pleasures of female looking – at men, other women, and the burgeoning attraction between them' as well as 'the knowing use of phallic iconography and *double entendres* in *Maurice* to melodramatise gay male desire' (2002: 191). This critical focus on gender and sexuality becomes especially relevant for the exploration of gay histories in the modern period film (as proposed by Dyer 2002), as well as queer readings of the classic woman's film constructed around intensely anti-naturalistic performances by actresses such as Gillian Anderson in *The House of Mirth* (Terence Davies, 2000) or Romola Garai in *Angel* (François Ozon, 2007).

The emergence of a post-heritage paradigm suggests a celebratory turn to postmodern cultural recycling and the aesthetic possibilities offered by pastiche in relation to the contemporary period film. Pamela Church Gibson (2000; 2002) notes a move away from the fetishisation of authenticity characteristic of the 1980s towards a hybrid aesthetic best represented in films since the mid-1990s by the mixture of genre conventions, anachronisms and high/low cultural references. This hybrid aesthetic includes social critique in *Persuasion* or *Gosford Park* (Robert Altman, 2001); eroticism, stylisation and heritage 'noir' in *The Wings of the Dove* (Iain Softley, 1997); harsh anti-heritage aesthetics of poverty and class struggle in *Jude*

(Michael Winterbottom, 1996) and meta-heritage approaches, as in the reflexive mise-en-scène of *A Cock and Bull Story* (Michael Winterbottom, 2005) (see Griem & Voigts-Virchow 2002). The post-heritage film has not only shed its reputation for quaintness and 'tastefulness' in favour of spectacle and postmodern games but also shows a renewed interest in imagining specific moments where present consciousness was formed.

This 'present-in-the-past' mode is at the basis of contemporary cinema's fascination with certain historical junctions that provide meaningful narratives to the contemporary cultural imagination. For Dianne F. Sadoff and John Kucich, the prominent return to the nineteenth century in postmodern culture is part of the search for defining cultural breaks, moments in which, as they put it, 'the present imagines itself to have been born and history for ever changed' (2000: x). This becomes apparent in the shifting tone and sense of instability (less reverential towards conventional notions of authenticity, bolder in its approach to the past as inextricably modern) that pervades the mise-en-scène of the nineteenth century in the second wave of heritage films that emerged since the mid-1990s. The fin-de-siècle aesthetics of *The Wings of the Dove* and its frank approach to class conflict and decadent sexuality (in contrast with the more familiar representation of 'repressed Victorians' still at large in *A Room with a View*) has prompted John McGowan to remark that 'the issue is not whether such a transitional time ever really existed, but that viewing any time as transitional is one of the hallmarks of the problematic of the modern' (2000: 12). The search for moments of crisis and change structures the backward projections of the heritage film within the stable narrative frame cemented by the reconstruction of place and period.

The understanding of retro-aesthetics as pastiche permits a closer examination of the formally reflexive aspects of the heritage film and the relation between emotion, consciousness and the politics of representation. For example, the deliberately artificial reconstruction of 1950s America in *Far from Heaven* (Todd Haynes, 2002) can be considered a departure from the compromised investment in authenticity (whether literary, historical or both) deployed by the heritage film (see Dyer 2007). As Richard Dyer notes, *Far from Heaven* is a pastiche, not of 1950s lifestyles but of the mirror held up by Hollywood melodrama to that historical period (in particular, the melodramas of Douglas Sirk). The pastiche of a genre embedded in film history allows the film to explore a historical structure of feeling delineated by what remains excluded rather than by what is made visible in the gap between then and now. In *Far from Heaven*, pastiche positions the audience at several removes from the conventions of the Hollywood tradition but this makes this domestic melodrama no less heart-wrenching. This use of pastiche to mobilise intense feeling through historically situated styles enables us, in the words of Dyer, 'to know ourselves affectively as historical beings' (2007: 180).

This understanding of pastiche is useful to address the self-reflexive turn in the period film of the 1990s and 2000s as well as the continuously approaching historical line of what constitutes a nation's heritage. The popular culture of the 1950s is at the centre of American cinema's exploration of its own political, artistic and social heritages. American films such as *Pleasantville* (Gary Ross, 1998), *Good Night, and Good Luck* (George Clooney, 2005), *The Notorious Betty Page* (Mary Harron, 2005), *Fur: An Imaginary Portrait of Diane Arbus* (Steven Shainberg, 2006) or the transatlantic co-productions *The Hours* (Stephen Daldry, 2002) and *Revolutionary Road* (Sam Mendes, 2008) knowingly exploit the familiar 1950s themes of suburban domesticity and the impact of television, as well as a robust film tradition of studio melodramas, in order to subvert clichéd images of the period as one of stability and prosperity. In the British context, cinema's retrospective look at the twentieth century has given visibility to alternative heritages that disrupt the dominant focus on the bourgeois milieu and literary narratives, such as the melancholic look on 1950s working-class experience in Mike Leigh's *Vera Drake* (2004), the recreation of the Manchester pop scene of the 1980s in *24 Hour Party People* (Michael Winterbottom, 2002) and *Control* (Anton Corbijn, 2007), or middle-class England on the brink of 1960s social change in *Nowhere Boy* (Sam Taylor-Wood, 2009) and *An Education* (Lone Scherfig, 2009). These period films use a different set of narrative conventions (the biopic or the memoir replacing the classical adaptation) and aesthetic devices (especially music and photography of the period) in much more self-conscious ways, intensifying the sense of affective closeness by tapping into a mass-mediated collective memory. In doing so, these films expand the possibilities of the heritage film to include a 'remembered' heritage located in popular culture, whilst contextualising the modern in direct tension with post-war social consensus in Britain.

The post-heritage film often returns to specific periods. For Sadoff and Kucich, rewritings of Victorian culture have flourished because 'the postmodern fetishises notions of cultural emergence, and because the nineteenth century provides multiple eligible sites for theorising such emergence' (2000: xv). This overdetermined re-interpretation of the past articulates some of the boldest literary adaptations of the second half of the 1990s. *Angels and Insects* (Philip Haas, 1995), *The Portrait of a Lady* or *Miss Julie* (Mike Figgis, 1999) deconstruct the class politics of the late Victorian era to produce a crude and pessimistic vision of social relations. The strident female garments in *Angels and Insects* offer a perfect example of (to extend Bruzzi's concept) the 'to-be-looked-at-ness' of costume to stress the constructedness of our ideas of the Victorian. In that film, positivist science and a Gothic tale of sexual in-breeding provide powerful metaphors for the reproduction of social structures of rank and class exclusion.

These films work hard at stressing the *presentness* of the adaptation rather than its *pastness*. For example, the Dogme-style handheld camera-work, split-screen techniques as well as the confined theatrical space and naturalistic performances create an atmosphere of heightened violence which builds through *Miss Julie*. In *The Portrait of a Lady*, a black-and-white credit sequence works as a non-narrative, modern prologue in which a gallery of young women dressed in casual 1990s clothes look confidently into the camera. This prologue is juxtaposed with the opening close-up (in colour) of Isabel Archer's (Nicole Kidman) anxious face, as she struggles to escape the narrow confines of the expectations placed on her as a young American heiress. To evoke Isabel's plight the film inserts set pieces that disrupt the reassuring framework of the realist mise-en-scène of period drama, most notably an oneiric sequence that shows Isabel's sexual fantasies and an experimental black-and-white short imitating the textures of primitive travelogues and surrealist cinema. These 'interferences' relocate the classical adaptation at the emergence of the film medium and literary modernism. Experiments like Campion's *Portrait of a Lady* and Figgis' *Miss Julie* incorporate heterogeneous sources and textures, suggesting that the genre has finally caught up with postmodern practice (see Church Gibson 2000).

And yet, despite multiple variations ('post-heritage', 'anti-heritage', 'alternative heritage', 'meta-heritage') that signal changes in sensibility, the heritage film remains, as Ginette Vincendeau points out, 'mainstream in terms of mise-en-scène' (2001a: xxiii), as it straddles art/auteur and mass cinema. The popularity of the heritage film largely depends on its ability to offer a readable mise-en-scène of the past, which allows for end-less variation but offers limited room for disruptive experimentation. The most adventurous examples of the genre (such as the above discussed films) performed poorly at the box office and received varying critical attention. Post-heritage labels reflect, however, the need to address the hybrid styles of the period film beyond the no longer satisfying association of period aesthetics with conservative nostalgia. Contextual changes do not automatically mean significant changes in form or narrative modes. Rather, it is the shifts in trends and sensibility, as well as the continuously expanding generic history of the heritage film that provide new models for the twenty-first century. The term 'post-heritage' may be most useful to refer not to the productivity or exhaustion of ongoing debates about the heritage film but to the changes in our affective relation with the past in ways that appeal directly to our present experience.

Feminine identities and the return of melodrama

The focus on gender has proved one of the most sustained and productive lines of investigation in the heritage film debate. As noted in chapter 1, the attention granted to the Gainsborough costume dramas by feminist scholars re-ignited the interest in a popular film culture that had been mar-ginalised in favour of the middlebrow heritage film. In studies of the British costume film in the 1930s and 1940s, Sue Harper (1994) and Pam Cook (1996) argue that the critical rejection of the Gainsborough studio films is intimately linked to biased views of gender and class. In these films, ornate and hyper-feminised costumes as well as elaborate sets produce an eroticised spectacle at odds with bourgeois notions of historical represen-tation, while sensational storylines stress feminine sexuality as a disrup-tive force. The underlining notions of genre and seriality exhibited by the Gainsborough melodramas, together with the films' 'unpalatable combi-nation of femininity, foreignness and lack of authenticity' (Cook 1996: 66) made them reviled objects in the eyes of the critical establishment but did not detract from their popularity. *The Wicked Lady* enjoyed a domestic suc-cess unparalleled by many of the quality dramas championed by middle-class critics. In this film the Restoration period acts as a familiar backdrop for a sensational melodrama about a reckless beauty (Margaret Lockwood) who, after seducing her best friend's fiancé, embarks on a career of crime

as a masked highway(wo)man. Transgressive romance, spectacular costumes and charismatic stars (Lockwood, Phyllis Calvert and James Mason)
enhance storylines that engage in fantasies of social mobility for women,
which account for the popularity of the genre during World War II and the
immediate post-war years.

This feminist reading of the escapist pleasures granted by the costume
film provides a powerful historical model for the retrieval of the popular
period drama.[2] As argued elsewhere (see Vidal 2005; 2007), the 1990s
period film often unearths women's histories through the return to pasts
steeped in fantasy. These returns to the past are filtered through the lens
of a postfeminist moment, in which the emphasis on female subjectivity
has been subsumed within the celebration of gendered forms of popular
culture. Young women in particular have become the privileged subject of
media cultures, which, as Yvonne Tasker and Diane Negra note (2007: 2),
naturalise aspects of feminism but also work to commodify it via the figure
of woman as empowered consumer.

Whereas *The Piano* and *Orlando* arguably open spaces for feminist
reflection in a postfeminist moment, the links between feminine identity,
romance and consumption come to the fore in later post-heritage films
informed by changing discourses on feminine agency. *The Duchess*, in
particular, is a significant example in a strand of costume melodramas
that maps anxieties about the postfeminist present onto a prefeminist
past. A biopic of eighteenth-century society lady Georgiana Spencer, the
film is a vehicle for Keira Knightley that follows her star-making turns
in Joe Wright's films *Pride and Prejudice* (2005) and *Atonement* (2007).
Knightley's Georgiana is a young and pliable heroine who, following her
mother's dictates, agrees to marry the older Duke of Devonshire (Ralph
Fiennes) in good faith. As the Duchess of Devonshire, Georgiana becomes
a celebrated society lady, a patron of the arts and a supporter of the liberal Whig party. However, in her private life she finds herself imprisoned
in a marriage solely engineered in order for her to produce a male heir.
Georgiana falls prey to a neglectful and abusive husband, and she is
deprived from female support when the Duke turns her friend Lady Bess
Foster (Hayley Atwell) into his in-house lover. Georgiana finds solace with
rising politician Charles Grey (Dominic Cooper), but gives him up when her
husband threatens to destroy his political career and to separate her from
her children.

Graham Fuller calls *The Duchess* 'a feminist tragedy that conforms perfectly to Monk's anti-heritage concept' (2008: 38). Not unlike the chilly *The Portrait of a Lady*, *The Duchess* is an anti-romance that situates a young woman at the centre of a 'house of fiction' tainted with power relations (Pidduck 2004: 63). In *The Duchess* the focus on costume articulates the ambiguity of the heroine's position. While endowing the character of Georgiana with a greater self-reflection than that afforded to the heroines of the Gainsborough melodramas, it also underscores the limits of her agency. On their wedding night the Duke proceeds to undress Georgiana for the unceremonious consummation of the marriage. To his complaint about the excessive 'complication' posed by women's clothes, Georgiana candidly replies that clothes are 'just our way of expressing ourselves, I suppose ... you have so many ways of expressing yourselves, whereas we must make do with our hats and our dresses'. This exchange is followed by a shot in which the camera tilts down close to Georgiana's bare back as her husband removes the corset. The close-up shows the marks infringed by the tight corset laces on her flesh. Georgiana constructs a persona for herself – dutiful wife and glamorous society hostess – that enables her to express herself publicly but oppresses her privately. This dramatic idea recurs in an exchange in which Georgiana discovers that her friend Bess suffers abuse at the hands of her husband by a red mark on her friend's neck, partially hidden by her bonnet. Likewise, Georgiana's wigs and hats are fashion statements and markers of wealth, yet one of her lowest points comes when her wig catches fire at a party, exposing her drunken state in front of other guests. The film thus constructs a double-edged discourse on clothes that highlights the function of costume as an outlet for sensuous pleasure, a means for empowerment and self-expression, as well as a tool for the control of women. While costume allows women to 'express themselves', it also hides their disenfranchisement.

In *The Duchess* the emphasis on a feminine construction of self through consumption confines the possibility of woman's revolt to the realm of the private. The socio-political past is cut down to the measure of a discourse on contemporary femininity and celebrity. History allows for a dramatisation of the public sphere that crushes feminine desires and aspirations. In this respect, the marketing of the film was dominated by references to Diana, Princess of Wales' turbulent private life in connection with her ancestor, the Duchess of Devonshire. French company Pathé launched an

Costume and excess: Georgiana attracts all the looks in *The Duchess*

aggressive advertising campaign with posters bearing the tag line 'there were three people in her marriage' inscribed over a close-up of a wide-eyed Knightley. The poster boldly highlights the star and the story as the film's key assets by means of a tight close-up that evokes the televisual mode of direct address rather than heritage pictorialism. Trailers included images of Diana juxtaposed with Knightley/Georgiana with the wording: 'two women related by ancestry … united by destiny … history repeats itself'. Pathé was eager to follow up its previous success with *The Queen*, which shows the interest of foreign investors in a high-concept British heritage picture (see Dawtrey 2008). In the bonus materials included in the UK DVD edition, the feature 'The Real Duchess' also stresses the parallels between Diana and Georgiana.[3] Amanda Foreman, author of the biography the film is based upon, presents the Duchess in the light of Diana's persona: a celebrity in her own time, Georgiana suffers from 'modern' addictions (bulimia, drugs, gambling) that stem from a precarious sense of self under pressure, her desire to please at all costs and her ability to make people feel 'important' and transmit warmth. Furthermore, the film portrays Georgiana as a candid target of the pro-Tory press (her affiliation to the Whig party is played only in terms of her relationship with Grey) and of satirical cartoonists, identified as a precedent to modern tabloids and paparazzi.

With regard to the monarchy film, Church Gibson points out that the public/private conflict cannot simply be resolved on a personal level. Solutions to personal problems often entail a constitutional crisis (2002: 35). As she goes on to note, this is what made Princess Diana's story so enthralling for the public and, one may add, so bankable for high-concept heritage films like *The Queen* and *The Duchess*. However, in *The Duchess* the dissociation of the personal from the political makes the film symptomatic of the constraints and contradictions negotiated by its ideological discourse. The motif of symmetrical long shots that place the Duke and the Duchess at opposite extremes of a long breakfasting table emphasises the oppressive nature of the marriage. Georgiana's humiliation is further reinforced when Bess joins the table, taking a seat between both spouses as the Duke's mistress and permanent fixture in the household. The mise-en-scène (reminiscent of the static compositions of Kubrick's *Barry Lyndon*) stresses rigidity and entrapment; it dramatises the progressive breaking of Georgiana's spirited resilience and the removal, one by one, of her sources of support. When Georgiana is impregnated by Grey, her liaison with the young Whig politician becomes a liability for his career and for her husband's credibility. Her emotional life thus threatens to spill into the public sphere but the impact of the loss of Grey's child is circumscribed to her point of view. Maternal melodrama irrupts momentarily into the controlled mise-en-scène in a sequence where Georgiana meets Grey's father in a deserted area outside the city to hand over her child. Stripped of her attributes of fame and wealth (she wears a plain print dress and no hat), Georgiana appears powerless and resigned to give up her illegitimate daughter Eliza, and breaks down as the baby girl is taken away. The setting, the barren landscape of a moor in the cold early morning light, intensifies her frailty and the extent of her loss.

The emotional violence of this scene makes the conciliatory happy ending of the film unsatisfactory and problematic. After losing lover and child, Georgiana is back on her feet and able to form a nurturing family circle with Bess and her children – a circle that, significantly, excludes the Duke. A bird's-eye shot of the women and children playing together in the gardens imposes a conventional sense of distance, whereas the end credits summarise the historical 'destiny' of the main characters and highlight the continuity of a matrilineal lineage (Eliza will name her own daughter Georgiana). This gesture towards the next generation of women recalls the mother-and-daughter ending of *Orlando* – with a difference. Whereas Potter's film ends on an optimistic note – the daughter will inherit and carry forward the gains of the feminist journey undertaken by her mother – the dénouement of *The Duchess* displaces Georgiana's trajectory of success, sacrifice and loss into the next generation. Rather than a narrative of progress, *The Duchess* suggests cyclical repetition whilst separating melodramatic emotion from social agency and political empowerment. The uplifting ending shows a happy Georgiana momentarily relieved from patriarchal pressures. However, the narrative does not challenge or subvert the patriarchal structures that underpin the education of women. The ending only highlights the film's unresolved ideological tensions in ways similar to the Hollywood maternal melodrama. By dismissing her struggle, the film leaves the historical heroine, physically and symbolically, out of history.

Such an ending serves the high-concept logic of the post-heritage film in the 2000s (the publicity links to Princess Diana's 'myth') and highlights the potential of the woman-centred monarchy film to become part of a profitable generic cycle. *The Other Boleyn Girl*, released in the UK six months before *The Duchess*, ends with a freeze frame showing the surviving daughter of Anne Boleyn as an innocent child destined to become the powerful Elizabeth I. This revelation appeals to the historical knowledge of the spectators but, above all, connects *The Other Boleyn Girl* to two previous films in the cycle: *Elizabeth* and *Elizabeth: The Golden Age*. The heritage film has become highly reflexive in its use of narrative and aesthetic elements that engage the spectator in a 'knowing' mode of address.

The Duchess follows in the steps of other monarchy films with an emphasis on young women. *Marie Antoinette* (2006) directed by a distinctive independent female auteur, Sofia Coppola, consciously highlights anachronisms (such as the use of rock and pop bands in the soundtrack) to emphasise the emotional journey of the queen as a modern heroine trapped in a historical fiction that she does not comprehend, and which concludes with her demise. The more conventional mise-en-scène of *The Young Victoria* (Jean-Marc Vallée, 2009) sheds the staid image of the nineteenth-century monarch, and presents her marriage to Albert, the Prince Consort, as a restrained love story mediated by letters, chess games and garden walks. By depicting their arranged marriage as a love union between two equals, this strangely quaint film isolates Victoria from her turbulent socio-political era. Although aesthetically very different, *Marie Antoinette* and *The Young Victoria* update the monarchy genre and target it at young female audiences by foregrounding a feminine perspective on teen romance as opposed to a feminist consciousness. These stories stress the fairytale motif of the princess in a golden cage, but the consciousness of her emotional isolation is tempered by the unlimited possibilities for consumption and self-display afforded by her royal status.

These popular costume films are symptomatic of a shift from the retrieval of women's histories and aesthetic experimentation of the 1990s post-heritage film to the commodification of feminism. By foregrounding the lifestyle of privileged young women, these costume films celebrate versions of femininity empowered by consumer and celebrity cultures. At the same time, *The Duchess, Marie Antoinette* and *The Young Victoria* deliver cautionary tales that depict women's choices undermined by emotional loss. In the last section of this chapter, we shall explore the potential of biopic to explore questions of agency, and re-imagine women's roles in history in a different way.

Girl with a Pearl Earring, the post-heritage biopic and the artist at work

The artist's biopic is one of the most popular strands of the heritage film. Film biographies of artists trade on the attractions granted by the often sensational fictions about the private lives of historical figures. These fictions are validated by the display of famous artworks and star performances that attempt to capture the mystery of creative genius. All these elements are part of *Girl with a Pearl Earring*, a mixture of biopic and romantic drama in which the focus on the artist shifts to a minor character in the margins of the grand narrative of art history. Discarding the 'life-story' structure, *Girl with a Pearl Earring* spins a romantic fiction about the production of an iconic Western artwork – Johannes Vermeer's painting *The Girl with the Pearl Earring* (1665) – and replaces the focus on male genius with an intriguing tale of female intervention. In the following pages I discuss the role of fictional characters in the contemporary biopic, and the ways in which *Girl with a Pearl Earring* reworks this genre to produce a meditation on feminine agency through the attention to what Pidduck calls the 'intimate contained spaces' of the heritage film (2004: 5).

Film biopics have often been accused of romanticising the figure of the artist. They commonly rely on biographical material as the source of meaning for the artwork, and present the artist as 'mad genius', justifying historical narratives that 'circle around categories of difference, otherness, excess' (Pollock 1980: 165). Costume and performance in *Girl with a Pearl Earring* sets the artist's personality apart in familiar ways. Colin

Firth's gloomy Vermeer embodies the artist as a difficult and introspective individual yet endowed with a unique vision. This cliché is indebted to star-driven formulas that hark back to the classic biopic. Thomas Elsaesser argues that the biopic addresses an imaginary consensus through the focus on the exceptional individual 'who is both within and outside given ideological discourses, who belongs to his age and in some sense transcends it' (1986: 26). This mythical construction shows, however, generic limits that are deeply historical. The contemporary biopic does not shy away from controversial cultural figures – such as the Marquis de Sade in *Quills* (Philip Kaufman, 2000) – or from exploring the artist's destructive behaviour. Ed Harris' tour-de-force performances as Jackson Pollock in *Pollock* (Ed Harris, 2000) and as Ludwig van Beethoven in *Copying Beethoven* (Agnieszka Holland, 2006) are a case in point, as they stress the artist's 'condition' as defined by misanthropy and isolation. However, the artist as impenetrable and larger-than-life figure often necessitates a narrative counterpoint, a witness to his genius who provides a narrative site of identification for the spectator. *Girl with a Pearl Earring* not only follows this convention, but pushes this peripheral role to the fore of the biopic's romantic fiction.

Peter Webber's film blurs the boundaries between biopic and 'biofantasy' (Custen 1992: 36) as it concentrates on the relationship between the male artist and a younger woman who becomes his model and assistant. The film starts with the arrival of Protestant maid Griet (Scarlett Johansson) to the Catholic Vermeer household, where she catches the painter's eye and is persuaded to model for him for what would become one of his best-known paintings. It is her point of view, rather than his, that structures the retelling of the artist's story. This idea is reinforced in publicity posters for the film: the two-shot of Griet/Johansson's and Vermeer/Firth's faces together conventionally suggests romance, but Griet's foreground position and her look at the spectator signal her prominent role in the film. Shifting the focus away from Vermeer, the gaze of the fictional character – the woman absent from history – channels the audience's engagement with the biographical fiction.

Romantic liaisons are a staple feature of the biopic, as they enhance the friction between the artist's public and private personas. They are also symptomatic of the gender bias characteristic of the genre. As Pidduck notes, 'male genius is frequently enabled by women who are muses (*Immortal*

Beloved, Shakespeare in Love) or nurturing mother figures (*Amadeus, Pandaemonium, Wilde*), but never creative agents in their own right' (2004: 93). When elevated to the main subject of the biopic, women artists are often locked in a relationship with a strong male mentor who, either as lover and/or tutor, casts a dramatic shadow over her life and work (for example, *Frida* (Julie Taymor, 2002)). However, by exploring emotional attachments that fall 'within the gaps between verifiable fact' (de Groot 2009: 217) the biopic also shapes historical narratives according to changing conceptions of gender relations and the position of the artist in society.

Copying Beethoven, a film with striking similarities to *Girl with a Pearl Earring*, is significant in this respect. Beethoven's documented use of various male assistants to transcribe his compositions is fictionalised into the composer's relationship with a single female copyist and music student, Anna Holtz (Diane Kruger), who assists him in the completion and première of the Ninth Symphony in Vienna in 1824. The film is narrated from the point of view of Anna, who also participates in the creation of the artwork through her labour. Whereas Anna's own ambitions as a composer provide the dramatic template for a fraught mentor/student relationship, the mise-en-scène places artistic creation next to forms of work associated with women's traditionally subservient roles. In the course of the film, Anna cleans, runs errands, bathes and nurses Beethoven – scenes that alternate with others of the young woman at the working desk. The painstaking task of copying the musical scores develops into an ongoing dialogue between composer and assistant, which leads to the centrepiece of the film: a twelve-minute sequence in which Anna *conducts* the stone-deaf Beethoven while he conducts the orchestra in the first public performance of the Ninth Symphony. Through whirlwind swish pans, dramatic zooms, inventive use of the raking focus and extreme close-ups edited to the rhythm and melodic patterns of the symphony, the extended sequence construes a moment of intense rapport between artist and copyist. As if possessed by a force beyond his control, Beethoven follows and mimics the authoritative gestures of his assistant who, during this key sequence, enables Beethoven's creative genius through the public performance of his work. Anna's 'invented' gestures do not substantially challenge the focus on the artist's genius; however, by stressing the performativity of the artwork as a historic event open to re-enactment and re-interpretation, the meanings of art are displaced from the focus on heroic male creativity to a narrative of female emancipation.

The post-heritage biopic turns from the life of the artist to the life of the artwork as an inexhaustible source of new fictions.[4] This supports the understanding of the biopic not as a full-blown, historically accurate portrait but as 'slices of lives, interventions into particular discourses, extended metaphors meant to suggest more that their limited time frames can convey' (Rosenstone 2007: 27). A transhistorical mode of significa-tion often takes precedence over the specificity of the period. In *Goya's Ghosts* (although namely a biopic of Spanish painter Francisco de Goya), the artist plays the role of witness to the downfall of one of his models, snatched and tortured by the Spanish Inquisition for her alleged Jewish origins. In *Quills* a barely literate laundress makes possible the circulation of the Marquis de Sade's incendiary prose by smuggling manuscripts out of the prison where he is confined and by transcribing his stories, of which she ends up becoming an indirect victim. In these films the artist loses his central position to fictional characters who, posing as unwitting histori-cal agents, serve ideological messages about the uses of art in times of political persecution. Both films are melodramas that politicise the artist's stance when faced with the curtailment of freedom of expression. Whether accomplice (as in *Copying Beethoven* or *Quills*) or muse (as in *Goya's Ghosts* or *Girl with a Pearl Earring*) the minor (in terms of the larger history) feminine character acts as a modern lens in the tunnel vision of historical reconstruction.

This revisionist approach to history is connected to changes in genre conventions and modes of production. *Girl with a Pearl Earring* stands as an example of the success of an industrial formula that uses culturally located artworks as part of its 'high concept' appeal but targets global audiences by enhancing the twin pleasures of period reconstruction and romance. As noted in chapter 2, this formula is connected to the de-centralisation of Hollywood, and the economy of multi-national co-productions. The incentive of tax breaks leads financial agents in major European industries such as the UK and France to team up with smaller players. *Girl with a Pearl Earring* was put together as a UK Film Council production set in the Dutch town of Delft, which was largely recreated in Luxembourg studios with the assistance of British and Dutch personnel (see Judell 2003). An example of a Europudding spoken in 'neutral' British English, the film is difficult to locate in national terms and yet it is instantly reminiscent of the

British heritage aesthetic, not least by the casting of Colin Firth as Vermeer. Significantly, this progressive de-nationalisation (and de-territorialisation) has its counterpoint on an increasing focus on style. As the international flow of funds, resources and creative personnel undermines cultural specificity, the heritage biopic remains culturally anchored – and instantly 'readable' – thanks to the central role of art (and its associations with a European heritage) and the consistency of its visual style.

In *Girl with a Pearl Earring* lighting and composition are used to create mood and atmosphere while forging visual links with the subject of the biopic. The opening sequence sets the tone of the film: in an interior setting, a Steadicam shot tracks forward through a corridor towards a threshold that leads into a room. The threshold double-frames the lone figure of Griet as she stands before a table, chopping and arranging vegetables on a plate. The scene is intercut with detail inserts of her hands at work, in shots that enhance the colours and textures of the vegetables, the patterns of the slices and the rhythm of Griet's repetitive gestures. Close-ups of her face and hunched shoulders emphasise the concentrated nature of manual work. The opening tracking shot is descriptive, rather than explicative. Griet is blocked off-centre and to the right of the frame, partially hidden at first by the hallway doors. The shot signals instead the world she inhabits. However, the closed composition, which places the young woman by the table and under a window, with natural light falling on her left, is designed to evoke the interiors and everyday scenes in Vermeer's works, hinting more generally to the tradition of still life painting and secular themes in Dutch Renaissance art. The scene triggers intertextual recognition, yet it does so through the perspective of one of Vermeer's anonymous models, whose point of view guides the spectator into the world of the film.

Painterly compositions have become a distinctive (and almost clichéd) marker of the heritage film since the 1990s. The increasingly composite nature of locations and the new possibilities afforded by digital postproduction permit the enhanced use of an eclectic mixture of painterly references as part of a unified approach to style. *Girl with a Pearl Earring* features aerial views and extreme long shots of Delft's town square and canals, which provide respite from the claustrophobic world of the household. A sequence in which Griet strolls with her suitor Pieter (Cillian Murphy) creates an opportunity for an establishing shot of a winter landscape bathed in golden light, strongly reminiscent of Dutch landscape painting. This hyperrealism, however, enhances the style of the film as close to pastiche: the citation of a painting style becomes a way of reproducing a worldview corresponding to the period. This style demands recognition, and therefore distance, but also draws the spectator into the illusion of a lived reality.

The closed compositions bring to the fore not only the physical but also the symbolic limits of the bounded worlds inhabited by the characters. When Griet is first sent to clean Vermeer's studio, the non-diegetic soundtrack and mise-en-scène highlight the weight of this moment in the narrative of the film. As she lifts slowly and with some effort each of the wooden panels covering the high windows in the studio, light floods in revealing a barely furnished room. A wall map, a wooden mannequin dressed with a yellow robe, a bright blue piece of cloth on a table, a canvas mounted on an easel and almost fully hidden by a curtain – each of these elements of mise-en-scène will play a role in the narrative, but the long shot and the perspectival composition act as visual cues to the Vermeer aesthetic. Standing at the centre of the shot and moving slowly from foreground to background, Griet introduces the spectator to the painter's 'separate' world (his wife and daughter remain, significantly, on the threshold) and *already* belongs in Vermeer's iconography.

This scene elicits not only the spectator's visual memory but his or her emotional involvement. As Charles Tashiro notes with regard to production design in historical films:

> Recognising the stylisation is part of the process of historical re-creation, since such recognition adds to the emotional distance between viewer and event ... By recognising our recognition, the film shares our perspective, implicating each in the other. Three distances – spatial, temporal, emotional – combine to create a strong sense of *presence.* (1998: 92; emphasis in original)

Stylised period reconstruction articulates a space of narrative potential which is, at the same time foreclosed by historical recognition. This exercise in pastiche serves, as Dyer has put it, to delineate the contours of a 'structure of feeling' not only by way of what it shows, but also what it cannot articulate, 'enabling and setting limits to the exercise of transhistorical sympathy' (2007: 177). *Girl with a Pearl Earring* derives its power to affect the spectator not just from the plausibility of its reconstruction, or

Stepping into the canvas: Griet lets the light in in *Girl with a Pearl Earring*

the consistency of its mood and tone ('the sense of *presence*'), but from the way in which objects and gestures play a role in the structure of feeling that makes the spectator deeply aware of the limits of the historical framework evoked in the film.

Griet's gaze both bears witness to the artist's genius and introduces a modern perspective on the myth of the artist which links the production of art to its socio-economic context. Unlike the conventionally feisty heroines of the costume film, Griet is an active observer but also a silent pawn in Vermeer's defensive negotiation of the pressures imposed on him by his powerful patron, his excitable wife and his meddling mother-in-law. Griet is subject to an increasingly uncomfortable friction with the upstairs world of the Catholic bourgeois family, rendered vividly by the sound design, which amplifies the constant noise disrupting the private, silent world of the Protestant maid. Romance eroticises the uneven power relations between artist and model, and the precious little dialogue exchanged between master and maid is subdued to the construction of the gaze to create moments of growing intimacy. Their intimacy culminates with Vermeer's piercing of Griet's ear so she can wear the large pearl earring. This distinctive detail in the famous canvas inspires an (unsubtle) symbolic male gesture that marks Griet's loss of innocence. This refashioning of Griet into the 'girl with a pearl earring' thus explains the historical 'enigma' posited by the woman in the painting through a familiar scenario of repression and desire.

However, the film delivers different and more intriguing pleasures in the margins of the conventional romance narrative – pleasures connected with the exploration and valorisation of women's gestures. Parallels are established between Griet's daily routine at the Vermeer household and the handling of the rare materials for the fabrication of the rich pigments of oils and lacquers for painting – a job Griet eventually takes over, working side by side with Vermeer. The preparation of food in the opening scene is replaced by the grinding and sieving of the colourful materials, a manual activity with an altogether different meaning that nevertheless requires the same precise, small gestures. Editing and sound design enhance Griet's hands and the tiny sounds made by the handling of the oils, as her face in close-up functions as a traditional signifier of inter-iority. The slow pace and discreet camerawork privileges observation and reaction, making room for the construction of feminine subjectivity in the imaginary vacant spaces left in the grand narrative of Vermeer's artistic creation. Upon looking at one of the paintings in progress in Vermeer's studio, Griet moves a chair placed in front of the dummy that stands in for the feminine figure in the canvas, thus 'unblocking' her. She later discovers that in the final painting the chair has disappeared from the composition. Her fictional intervention is incorporated into the layers of signification accrued by the painting, altering its meaning within the structure of feeling set up by the film.

Such moments make up the highlights of a narrative visually organised around two contrasting motifs: the (clichéd) performance of male genius versus the 'modern', invented gestures of female intervention, which articulate the relationship between the painter and his would-be model. Performances are one of the main attractions of the popular biopic, carrying some of the un-ironic emotional intensity attached to pastiche. Vermeer's intense glances are often shielded by the internal lines within the frame as he peeks at Griet around the edge of the easel, or partially hidden by a threshold. While his gaze is oblique and retains a sense of mystery, hers is inquisitive and straightforward. Lingering close-ups underline her position as silent observer of the growing drama of jealousy and manipulation unfolding at the Vermeer household. The actors' performances are, however, dependent on their construction through costume and other elements of mise-en-scène. Firth embodies Vermeer as a brooding presence, shunning the over-the-top performances often found in star-driven biopics (Harris in *Copying Beethoven* is an example of this). However, details like the wig donned by the male star are constantly on the brink of becoming 'excessive' signifiers: awkward yet 'necessary' elements of mise-en-scène that transform historical verisimilitude into (intertextual) cliché.

Woman at work: Griet prepares the painting oils in *Girl with a Pearl Earring*

Discussing the prominent fringes that adorn the actors' 'Roman' foreheads in the Hollywood version of *Julius Caesar* (Joseph L. Mankiewicz, 1953), Roland Barthes identifies the semiotic nature of historical verisimilitude as an 'ethic of signs' that leads him to mistrust what he calls the ambiguous 'intermediate sign': 'the sign that presents itself at once as intentional and irrepressible, artificial and natural, manufactured and discovered ... equally afraid of simple reality and of total artifice' (2000: 28). The 'wig' stands for the performance of authenticity in the heritage film, a sign that both seals and disrupts the fiction as it unveils heritage authenticity as pure 'heritage style'. Neither self-effacing nor overtly camp, the artist's wig draws attention to the limits of consensual (middlebrow) realism at a given point in time. And yet, paradoxically, such clichéd performance of male genius reinforces the illusion of naturalism attached to the fictional female character's anachronistic gestures. Pastiche thus serves authenticity and emotion.

The contemporary heritage film is the product of transnational arrangements, with visual style becoming the vehicle for both narrative identification and intertextual recognition. In *Girl with a Pearl Earring* the reflection on the nation is brushed aside by a narrative that explores the meanings of the artwork in order to offer a popular reworking of history 'from below' with an emphasis on issues of gender, class and creativity. Through Griet the nuts-and-bolts of social history enter the game of intertextuality and historicity at work in the representation of European heritages. Griet's historically implausible but affective gestures are central to a cultural narrative that seeks to explain the European artistic heritage to a contemporary audience.

As the markers of national identity fade away and the generic markers become more visible, the biopic increasingly situates its 'authenticity' in relation to painstaking detail and a melodramatic mode of address. Period authenticity thus becomes a key generic trait deployed for dramatic effect, and visual affect. *Girl with a Pearl Earring* was quickly followed by a strand of biopics marketed as romantic period dramas, including *Finding Neverland* (Marc Forster, 2004), *Miss Potter* (Chris Noonan, 2006) and *Becoming Jane*. Like Webber's film, these films exploit a well-defined heritage iconography and strategically combine American stars with supporting casts of international 'quality' players. Significantly, they all re-imagine the writer's biography through his/her works. *Becoming Jane* dramatises Jane Austen's life as a pastiche of her work with Austen as the quintessential 'Austenian' heroine, whereas *Finding Neverland* mixes fantasy scenes inspired by Peter Pan with the relationship of James Barry with the Llewelyn Davies family. In these biopics the artist is not only re-imagined as the protagonist of his/her own fictions, but also relocated to small-scale, domestic and thoroughly feminised worlds attentive to the nuances of gesture. Rather than a heroic enterprise, the making of art is presented as a craft inspired by everyday details and events. More importantly, art helps construct self-enclosed worlds of imagination that give expression to mourning. While remaining safely confined within bourgeois notions of the artist, these popular biopics forsake the myth of the extra-ordinary individual in favour of creativity as a way of overcoming loss and bereavement, a theme also revisited in *Girl with a Pearl Earring* through Griet's sense of isolation when forced to leave the family home for the hostile environment of the Vermeer household.

The narrow scope of the post-heritage biopic on pastiche and emotion cannot encompass the wider contextual, aesthetic or political reflection on the crucial historical periods represented. However, it is arguably the imaginative remaking of European high culture into popular narratives built upon the many lives of the artwork that informs the pleasures of repetition and allows for spaces of generic variation to emerge in the contemporary biopic. Through a narrative around the imagined relationship between the artist and the in-house maid forced to act as his model, the portrait of the artist opens up to the exploration of the class and gender implications that 'explain' the artwork for a contemporary audience. The tension between the vantage points of artist and model is also the tension between the monological and ultimately mythical narrative of the biopic, and a more dialogical retelling of cultural histories. The biopic thus reinvents itself as a genre that promotes participatory fantasies about the past.

Notes

1. For a related formulation of this idea, see Garrett (1995) on 'counter-memory'.
2. This model has been evoked in new contexts of interpretation such the fashioning of a diasporic Jewish identity in the Scotland-set melodrama *The Governess*. See Martin-Jones (2009).
3. 'Making-of documentary'. *The Duchess*. DVD. Pathé/Twentieth-Century Fox Home Entertainment, 2009.
4. Thanks to João Laia and Suzanne Daurat for this suggestion.

AFTERWORD: TRADITION AND CHANGE

Almost twenty years on, the heritage film debate appears as the symptom of the problematic negotiation of Englishness in British cinema, and of British cinema in international markets. The relation between these terms underwent remarkable changes in the 1990s and the 2000s, which suggests the fluidity of a genre and the complexities of a debate whose central tenets have too often been oversimplified in favour of, as Sue Harper has put it, 'a clear explanatory model that is attractive because it makes things look simple, and because it confers a pleasing symmetry onto the seeming chaos of cultural forms' (2004: 140). Implicit (and sometimes explicit) in the discussion lie the politics of taste that inform the reception of the heritage film and its unspoken status as the 'bad object' *par excellence* in 1990s academic film studies. Dismissed as formally and ideologically unadventurous, the heritage film seemed neither popular enough nor sufficiently 'arty' to warrant serious attention. And yet this genre makes a strong case for the irrelevance of such binary opposition in contemporary cinema, as it asserts its place as one of the most durable European genres and a thriving area of research in its own right.

In 2005 and 2006 two vastly different British heritage films were released within a few months of each other. They represent two complementary sides of the genre. Joe Wright's *Pride and Prejudice*, a British production with American and French funding, culminated a ten-year cycle of highly successful Jane Austen adaptations, initiated by the BBC serial *Pride and Prejudice*. The feature film of *Pride and Prejudice* was a lavish affair, preceded by a promotional UK poster that recalls Ang Lee and Emma Thompson's 'classic' *Sense and Sensibility*. The poster shows a close-up of a dreamy Elizabeth Bennet against a blurred natural background, with

Darcy behind her, looking on melancholically. The film opens with a long shot of the peaceful English countryside bathed in golden sunlight. A series of exterior shots follow a quick-paced Elizabeth as she walks, book in hand, towards the Bennets' modest but picturesque family home. She is first shown reading and walking, until she approaches the house. The camera then glides inside to meet the four Bennet sisters in a vignette of lively domesticity, and then picks up Elizabeth again, as she stops outside a window. A point-of-view shot shows her parents inside, isolated within this double-framing device. Her agitated mother communicates an important piece of news to her indifferent father: the arrival of new tenants at Netherfield Park. Elizabeth smiles and goes into the house. This gesture acknowledges not only her familiarity with the scene, but ours as well.

The opening does not so much introduce the plot and its main characters as it condenses an array of heritage tropes in a visually eloquent manner. The pastoral landscape, the soft piano theme and the centrality of the period house stay faithful to the established iconography of the genre, while the widescreen cinematography and smooth, mobile camerawork asserts this new version of the Austen classic as emphatically cinematic. The literary word is replaced by self-conscious references to reading and looking, two activities that present Elizabeth as the protagonist, the reader and the spectator of her own story. Austen's novel is thus condensed into a series of recurrent figures and meanings attached to a genre that functions as a generative template for new films. *Pride and Prejudice* expands the boundaries of its genre but does it from its very centre, retracing its steps with a clear sense of narrative self-consciousness and an auteurist sensibility.

Familiar scenes: self-conscious mise-en-scène and the knowing spectator in *Pride and Prejudice*

The credit sequence of *A Cock and Bull Story* makes for interesting comparison. The credits roll over a fixed, straight-on long shot of a typically sumptuous manor house, and yet the sequence evokes three intertexts that are far from the conventional heritage film: the experimental literary adaptation (the film is based on the famously self-reflexive *The Life and Opinions of Tristram Shandy, Gentleman*, by Laurence Sterne); the avant-garde cinema of Peter Greenaway (the sequence borrows the main theme by Michael Nyman for the soundtrack of *The Draughtsman's Contract*); and British television comedy, introduced by the presence of popular stand-up and television comedian Steve Coogan in the multiple roles of Tristram Shandy, Walter Shandy and Steve Coogan. This shaggy-dog story about the impossibility of adapting Tristam Shandy also works as an extended reflection on the impossibility of making anything close to a pure heritage film, as obstacles of various kinds hamper the making of the film adaptation, including financial difficulties, production constraints, star egos and interfering opinions by persons extraneous to the set. Such obstacles provide layer upon layer of interferences but also work as enriching intertextual connections that transform the heritage film into a comic mirror of the reality of a precarious, yet resourceful, British industry.

While *Pride and Prejudice* dwells on the sensations attached to recognition and nostalgia, *A Cock and Bull Story* undercuts the stasis of the *mise-en-scène* of the past by happily mixing heterogeneous textures and elements. Yet both films still place typical heritage pleasures at their very centre: the use of visual spectacle to construe emotion in *Pride and Prejudice* and literate dialogue and exuberant performances in *A Cock and Bull Story*. In so doing, these films continue to refer to a tradition embedded in the principles of realism and quality, once extolled as the pillars of British national cinema. The contemporary heritage film may arguably function as a cinema against the grain, offering a reassuring retreat from the barrage of unsettling views that emerge from what has been called a post-British cinema (see Brown 2009), that is, a cinema that resists stable themes of national identity through a *dis-location* in form and content. However, a different starting point for this book could have been the consideration of the ways in which the post-national already forms part of the British heritage film. For example, *The Last King of Scotland*, a Scottish production released in the same year as *The Queen*, casts an ironic look at the 1970s and onto myths of Scottishness in order to present a disturb-

Comic wit and layered reflexivity: Tristram Shandy/Steve Coogan addresses the audience in
A Cock and Bull Story

ing image of Britishness abroad. *The Last King of Scotland* is arguably
the Hyde to *The Queen*'s Dr Jekyll: the monstrous reverse of the benign
iconographies of nation and tradition associated with the contemporary
monarchy film, which links the present to a past of colonialism and intervention in the affairs of other countries. All four films stand out among the
defining British films of the decade and suggest the continuous relevance
of the heritage film in connection with a wider range of forms and representations than those previously acknowledged in the early stages of the
heritage film debate.

At the risk of initiating threads that this book cannot fully pursue, and
of invoking methodological problems that cannot be properly resolved
within its limited space, I have attempted to assess the representations
of the past offered by the heritage film within the continuously expanding
boundaries of the genre: *The Queen* suggests ways in which the iconography of the monarchy film provides a structuring template for new representations of nation; *Joyeux Noël* mobilises the reconstruction of the traumatic
past towards the construction of a common European future; and *Girl with
a Pearl Earring* throws light over the dynamics of gender, creativity and
romance in the popular heritage biopic. The cinematic pleasures offered by
these and many other films still relate to the terms of tradition and change
outlined in the initial heritage debates. These cinematic works attest to
the richness of the genre, while suggesting new directions in which it may
develop in coming years.

FILMOGRAPHY

Films

1492 Christophe Colomb (*1492 Conquest of Paradise,* Ridley Scott, UK/
   France/Spain, 1992)
24 Hours Party People (Michael Winterbottom, UK, 2002)
Aimée und Jaguar (*Aimée and Jaguar,* Max Färberböck, Germany, 1999)
Amadeus (Milos Forman, USA, 1984)
Amour de Swann, Un (*Swann in Love,* Volker Schlöndorff, France/West
   Germany, 1984)
Angel (François Ozon, UK/Belgium/France, 2007)
Angels and Insects (Philip Haas, USA/UK, 1995)
Anglaise et le duc, L' (*The Lady and the Duke,* Éric Rohmer, France, 2001)
Anna Karenina (Bernard Rose, USA,1997)
Atonement (Joe Wright, UK/France, 2007)
Auberge espagnole, L' (*Pot Luck,* Cédric Klapisch, France/Spain, 2002)
Baader Meinhof Komplex, Der (*The Baader Meinhof Complex,* Uli Edel,
   Germany/France/Czech Republic, 2008)
Babettes gæstebud (*Babette's Feast,* Gabriel Axel, 1987)
Barry Lyndon (Stanley Kubrick, UK/USA, 1975)
Basic Instinct (Paul Verhoeven, USA, 1992)
Beau Brummell (Curtis Bernhardt, USA, 1954)
Becoming Jane (Julian Jarrold, UK/Ireland, 2007)
Belle Époque (Fernando Trueba, 1992)
Bostonians, The (James Ivory, UK/USA, 1984)

Boy in the Striped Pyjamas, The (Mark Herman, UK/USA, 2008)
Bride and Prejudice (Gurinder Chadha, UK/USA, 2004)
Brideshead Revisited (Julian Jarrold, UK/Italy/Morocco, 2008)
Bridget Jones's Diary (Sharon Maguire, UK/Ireland/France, 2001)
Buongiorno, notte (*Good Morning, Night*, Marco Bellocchio, Italy, 2003)
Capitaine Conan (Bertrand Tavernier, France, 1996)
Captain Corelli's Mandolin (John Madden, UK/France/USA, 2001)
Caravaggio (Derek Jarman, UK, 1986)
Carrington (Christopher Hampton, UK/France, 1995)
Chambre des officiers, La (*The Officer's Ward*, François Dupeyron, France,
    2001)
Chariots of Fire (Hugh Hudson, UK, 1981)
Charlotte Gray (Gillian Armstrong, UK/Australia/Germany, 2001)
Château de ma mère, Le (*My Mother's Castle*, Yves Robert, France, 1990)
Chocolat (Lasse Hallström, UK/USA, 2001)
Chronicles of Narnia: Prince Caspian, The (Andrew Adamson, UK/USA,
    2008)
Chronicles of Narnia: The Lion, the Witch and the Wardrobe, The (Andrew
    Adamson, UK/USA, 2005)
Cock and Bull Story, A (Michael Winterbottom, UK, 2005)
Comrades (Bill Douglas, UK, 1986)
Control (Anton Corbijn, UK/USA/Australia/Japan, 2007)
Copying Beethoven (Agnieszka Holland, USA/Germany/Hungary, 2006)
Cousin Bette (Des McAnuff, UK/USA, 1998)
Cyrano de Bergerac (Jean-Paul Rappenau, France, 1990)
Damned United, The (Tom Hooper, UK/USA, 2009)
Dangerous Beauty (Marshall Herskovitz, USA, 1998)
Danton (Andrzej Wajda, France/Poland/West Germany, 1983)
Destinées sentimentales, Les (*Sentimental Destinies*, Olivier Assayas,
    France/Switzerland, 2000)
Distant Voices, Still Lives (Terence Davies, UK, 1988)
Dr Zhivago (David Lean, USA/UK, 1965)
Draughtsman's Contract, The (Peter Greenaway, UK, 1982)
Duchess, The (Saul Dibb, UK/Italy/France, 2008)
Education, An (Lone Scherfig, UK, 2009)
Elizabeth (Shekhar Kapur, UK, 1998)
Elizabeth: The Golden Age (Shekhar Kapur, UK/France/Germany, 2007)

Emma (Douglas McGrath, UK/USA, 1996)

Enemy at the Gates (Jean-Jacques Annaud, USA/Germany/UK/Ireland, 2001)

English Patient, The (Anthony Minghella, USA/UK, 1996)

Espinazo del diablo, El (*The Devil's Backbone*, Guillermo del Toro, Spain/ Mexico, 2001)

Espíritu de la colmena, El (*The Spirit of the Beehive*, Víctor Erice, Spain, 1973)

Fantasmas de Goya, Los (*Goya's Ghosts,* Milos Forman, USA/Spain, 2006)

Far from Heaven (Todd Haynes, USA, 2002)

Finding Neverland (Marc Forster, USA/UK, 2004)

Flame in the Streets (Roy Ward Baker, UK, 1961)

Fort Saganne (Alain Corneau, France, 1984)

Four Weddings and a Funeral (Mike Newell, UK, 1994)

Frida (Julie Taymor, USA/Canada/Mexico, 2002)

Frost/Nixon (Ron Howard, USA/UK/France, 2008)

Fur: An Imaginary Portrait of Diane Arbus (Steven Shainberg, USA, 2006)

Gabrielle (Patrice Chéreau, French/Italy/Germany, 2005)

Gandhi (Richard Attenborough, UK/India, 1982)

Germinal (Claude Berri, France/Belgium/Italy, 1993)

Girl with a Pearl Earring (Peter Webber, UK/Luxembourg, 2003)

Gloire de mon père, La (*My Father's Glory*, Yves Robert, France, 1990)

Go-Between, The (Joseph Losey, UK, 1970)

Gold Diggers, The (Sally Potter, UK, 1983)

Good Night, and Good Luck (George Clooney, USA, 2005)

Good-bye Lenin! (Wolfgang Becker, Germany, 2003)

Gosford Park (Robert Altman, UK/USA, 2001)

Gothic (Ken Russell, UK, 1986)

Governess, The (Sandra Goldbacher, UK, 1998)

Grande illusion, La (Jean Renoir, France, 1937)

Henry V (Laurence Olivier, UK, 1944)

History Boys, The (Nicholas Hytner, UK, 2006)

Hours, The (Stephen Daldry, USA/UK, 2002)

House of Mirth, The (Terence Davies, UK/USA, 2000)

House of the Spirits, The (Bille August, Portugal/Germany/Denmark, USA, 1993)

Howards End (James Ivory, UK/Japan, 1992)

Hunger (Steve McQueen, UK/Ireland, 2008)
Idi i smotri (*Come and See*, Elem Klimov, USSR, 1985)
Immortal Beloved (Bernard Rose, UK/USA, 1994)
Indochine (*Indochina*, Régis Wargnier, France, 1992)
Inglorious Basterds (Quentin Tarantino, USA/Germany, 2008)
Iris (Richard Eyre, UK, 2001)
Jag är Dina (*I Am Dina*, Ole Bornedal, Sweden/France/Norway/Germany/
     Denmark, 2002)
Jane Austen Book Club, The (Robin Swicord, USA, 2007)
Jassy (Bernard Knowles, UK, 1947)
Jean de Florette (Claude Berri, France/Switzerland/Italy, 1986)
Joseon namnyeo sangyeoljisa (*Untold Scandal,* Je-yong Lee, South Korea,
     2003)
Joyeux Noël (*Merry Christmas,* Christian Carion, France/ Germany/ UK/
     Belgium/ Romania, 2005)
Jude (Michael Winterbottom, UK, 1996)
Julius Caesar (Joseph L. Mankiewicz, USA, 1953)
Jurassic Park (Steven Spielberg, USA, 1993)
Klimt (Raoul Ruiz, Austria/France/Germany/UK, 2006)
Laberinto del fauno, El (*Pan's Labyrinth*, Guillermo del Toro, Spain/
     Mexico/USA, 2006)
Land and Freedom (*Tierra y libertad,* Ken Loach, UK/ Spain/ Germany/
     Italy, 1995)
Last King of Scotland, The (Kevin Macdonald, UK, 2006)
Last of England, The (Derek Jarman, UK, 1987)
Leben der Anderen, Das (*The Lives of Others,* Florian Henckel von
     Donnersmarck, Germany, 2006)
Long dimanche de fiançailles, Un (*A Very Long Engagement*, Jean-Pierre
     Jeunet, France/USA, 2004)
Lord of the Rings, The (Peter Jackson, USA/New Zealand/Germany,
     2001-2003)
Luzhin Defence, The (Marleen Gorris, UK/France, 2000)
Madness of King George, The (Nicholas Hytner, UK, 1994)
Madonna of the Seven Moons (Arthur Crabtree, UK, 1944)
Man in Grey, The (Leslie Arliss, UK, 1943)
Manon des sources (Claude Berri, France/Switzerland/Italy 1986)
Mansfield Park (Patricia Rozema, UK, 1999)

Marie Antoinette (Sofia Coppola, USA/France/Japan, 2006)

Maurice (James Ivory, UK, 1987)

Messenger: The Story of Joan of Arc, The (Luc Besson, France, 1999)

Millions Like Us (Frank Launder and Sidney Gilliat, UK, 1943)

Miss Julie (Mike Figgis, UK, 1999)

Miss Potter (Chris Noonan, UK/USA 2006)

Mrs Brown (John Madden, UK/Ireland/USA, 1997)

Muertos de risa (*Dying of Laughter*, Álex de la Iglesia, Spain, 1999)

My Brilliant Career (Gillian Armstrong, Australia, 1979)

Name der Rose, Der (*The Name of the Rose*, Jean-Jacques Annaud, France/
Italy/West Germany, 1986)

Notes on a Scandal (Richard Eyre, UK, 2006)

Notorious Betty Page, The (Mary Harron, USA, 2005)

Notting Hill (Roger Michell, UK/USA, 1999)

Nowhere Boy (Sam Taylor-Wood, UK/Canada, 2009)

Nuovo Cinema Paradiso (*Cinema Paradiso*, Giuseppe Tornatore, Italy/
France, 1988)

Ogniem i mieczem (*With Fire and Sword*, Jerzy Hoffman, Poland, 1999)

Oliver Twist (Roman Polanski, UK/Czech Republic/France/Italy, 2005)

Onegin (Martha Fiennes, UK/USA, 1999)

Orlando (Sally Potter, UK/Russia/France/Italy/Netherlands, 1992)

Other Boleyn Girl, The (Justin Chadwick, UK/USA, 2008)

Otros, Los (*The Others*, Alejandro Amenábar, USA/Spain/France/Italy,
2001)

Pacte des loups, Le (*Brotherhood of the Wolf*, Christophe Gans, France,
2001)

Pan Tadeusz (*Pan Tadeusz: The Last Foray in Lithuania*, Andrzej Wajda,
Poland/France, 1999)

Passage to India, A (David Lean, UK/USA, 1984)

Paths of Glory (Stanley Kubrick, USA, 1957)

Pelle Erobreren (*Pelle the Conqueror*, Bille August, Denmark/Sweden,
1987)

Perfume: The Story of a Murderer (Tom Tykwer, Germany/France/Spain/
USA, 2006)

Persuasion (Roger Michell, UK/USA/France, 1995)

Pianist, The (Roman Polanski, France/Poland/Germany/UK, 2002)

Piano, The (Jane Campion, Australia/New Zealand/France, 1993)

Pleasantville (Gary Ross, USA, 1998)

Pollock (Ed Harris, USA, 2000)

Portrait of a Lady, The (Jane Campion, USA/UK, 1996)

Postino, Il (*The Postman*, Michael Radford, Italy/France, 1994)

Pride and Prejudice (Joe Wright, UK/France, 2005)

Private Life of Henry VIII, The (Alexander Korda, UK, 1933)

Putain du roi, La (*The King's Whore*, Axel Corti, Austria/France/Italy/
    Britain, 1990)

Queen, The (Stephen Frears, UK/France, 2006)

Quills (Philip Kaufman, USA/Germany/UK, 2000)

Reader, The (Stephen Daldry, UK, 2008)

Reine Margot, La (*Queen Margot*, Patrice Chéreau, French/Italy/Germany,
    1994)

Remains of the Day, The (James Ivory, UK/USA, 1993)

Revolutionary Road (Sam Mendes, USA/UK, 2008)

Romeo + Juliet (Baz Luhrmann, USA, 1996)

Room with a View, A (James Ivory, 1986)

Saint-Cyr (*The King's Daughters*, Patricia Mazuy, France/Germany/
    Belgium, 2000)

Salvador (*Puig Antich*) (Manuel Huerga, Spain/UK, 2006)

Sammy and Rosie Get Laid (Stephen Frears, UK, 1987)

Sapphire (Basil Dearden, UK, 1959)

Saving Private Ryan (Steven Spielberg, USA, 1998)

Schindler's List (Steven Spielberg, USA, 1993)

Sense and Sensibility (Ang Lee, USA/UK, 1995)

Shakespeare in Love (John Madden, USA/UK, 1998)

Sibirskij Tsiryulnik (*The Barber of Siberia*, Nikita Mihaljkov, Russia/
    France/Italy/Czech Republic, 1998)

Sonnenallee (*Sun Alley*, Leander Haussmann, Germany, 1999)

Sunshine (István Szabó, Germany/Austria/Canada/Hungary, 1999)

Sylvia (Christine Jeffs, UK, 2003)

Temps retrouvé, Le (*Time Regained*, Raoul Ruiz, France/Italy/Portugal,
    1999)

Tess (Roman Polanski, France/UK, 1979)

That Hamilton Woman/Lady Hamilton (Alexander Korda, UK, 1941)

Thriller (Sally Potter, UK, 1979)

Tom Jones (Tony Richardson, UK, 1963)

Torremolinos 73 (Pablo Berger, Spain/Denmark, 2003)

Untergang, Der (*Downfall*, Oliver Hirschbiegel, Germany/Italy/Austria, 2004)

Valmont (Milos Forman, France/USA, 1989)

Vanity Fair (Mira Nair, UK/USA, 2004)

Vera Drake (Mike Leigh, UK/France/New Zealand, 2004)

Veuve de St Pierre, La (*The Widow of St Pierre*, Patrice Leconte, France/Canada, 2000)

Victoria the Great (Herbert Wilcox, UK, 1938)

Vidocq (Pitof, France, 2001)

Vie et rien d'autre, La (*Life and Nothing But*, Bertrand Tavernier, France, 1989)

Violon rouge, Le (*The Red Violin*, François Girard, Canada/Italy/UK 1998)

Vita è bella, La (*Life is Beautiful*, Roberto Benigni, Italy, 1997)

Where Angels Fear to Tread (Charles Sturridge, UK, 1991)

Wicked Lady, The (Leslie Arliss, UK, 1945)

Wings of the Dove, The (Iain Softley, USA/UK, 1997)

Young Mr Pitt, The (Carol Reed, UK, 1942)

Young Victoria, The (Jean-Marc Vallée, UK/USA, 2009)

Zwartboek (*Black Book*, Paul Verhoeven, Netherlands/Germany/Belgium, 2006)

Television

Big Brother, Channel Four (Bazal/Channel Four/Endemol Entertainment UK, 2000-2010)

Bleak House, BBC (BBC/WGBH/Deep Indigo Productions, 2005)

Brideshead Revisited, ITV (Granada, 1981)

Culloden, BBC (BBC, 1964)

Daniel Deronda, BBC (BBC/WGBH, 2002)

Deal, The, Channel Four (Granada, 2003)

Devil's Whore, The, Channel Four (Company Pictures/HBO/Power, 2008)

Elizabeth I, Channel Four (Company Pictures/Channel4/HBO, 2005)

Emma, BBC (BBC Drama Productions, 2009)

Emma, ITV (Meridian/A&E, 1996)

Fingersmith, BBC (Sally Head Productions/BBC, 2005)

Fortunes and Misfortunes of Moll Flanders, The, ITV (Granada/WGBH, 1996)

Inspector Morse, ITV (Zenith Productions/Carlton Television, 1987-2000)
Jewel in the Crown, The, ITV (Granada, 1984)
Little Dorrit, BBC (BBC/WGBH, 2008)
Longford, Channel 4 (Channel Four/Granda/HBO, 2006)
Lost in Austen, ITV (Mammoth Screen, 2008)
Lost Prince, The, BBC (TalkBack/BBC/WGBH, 2003)
Love Again, BBC (BBC/World Productions, 2003)
Mansfield Park, ITV (Company Pictures/WGBH, 2007)
Miss Austen Regrets, BBC (BBC/WGBH, 2008)
Northanger Abbey, ITV (Granada/ITV/WGBH, 2007)
Other Boleyn Girl, The, BBC (BBC, 2003)
Our Friends in the North, BBC (BBC, 1996)
Persuasion, ITV (Clerkenwell Films/WGBH, 2007)
Pride and Prejudice, BBC (BBC/A&E, 1995)
Prime Suspect, ITV (Granada, 1991–2006)
Sense and Sensibility, BBC (BBC, 2008)
Special Relationship, The, BBC (Rainmark Films/HBO Films/BBC Films, 2010)
Tenant of Wildfell Hall, The, BBC (BBC/CBC/WGBH, 1996)
Tipping the Velvet, BBC (Sally Head Productions, 2002)
Tudors, The, BBC (Peace Arch Entertainment/Showtime Networks/Reveille Productions/Working Title Films/CBC/Bórd Scannán na hÉireann/PA Tudors/TM Productions, 2007- 2010)
Vanity Fair, BBC (BBC/A&E, 1998)

BIBLIOGRAPHY

Austin, Guy (2008) *Contemporary French Cinema,* 2nd edn. Manchester: Manchester University Press.

Austin, James F. (2004) 'Digitizing Frenchness in 2001: On a "Historic" Moment in the French Cinema', *French Cultural Studies,* 15, 281–99.

Balio, Tino (1998) 'The Art Film Market in the New Hollywood', in Geoffrey Nowell-Smith (ed.) *Hollywood and Europe: Economics, Culture, National Identity 1945–95.* London: British Film Institute, 63–73.

Barr, Charles (1986) 'Introduction: Amnesia and Schizophrenia', in Charles Barr (ed.) *All Our Yesterdays: 90 Years of British Cinema.* London: British Film Institute, 1–29.

Barthes, Roland (2000 [1957]) *Mythologies.* London: Vintage.

Bergfelder, Tim (2000) 'The Nation Vanishes: European Co-productions of the 1950s and 1960s', in Mette Hjort and Scott Mackenzie (eds) *Cinema and Nation.* London: Routledge, 139–52.

____ (2005) 'National, Transnational or Supranational Cinema?: Rethinking European Film Studies', *Media, Culture and Society,* 27, 3, 315–31.

Beumers, Birgit (2000) '*Sibirskii tsiriul'nik (The Barber of Siberia)*', in Jill Forbes and Sarah Street (eds) *European Cinema: An Introduction.* Basingtoke: Palgrave, 195–206.

Blandford, Steve (2007) *Film, Drama and the Break-up of Britain.* Bristol: Intellect.

Brandstrup, Pil Gundelach and Eva Novrup Redvall (2005) 'Breaking the Borders: Danish Coproductions in the 1990s', in Andrew Nestingen and Trevor G. Elkington (eds) *Transnational Cinema in a Global North.*

Detroit: Wayne State University Press, 141–63.

Brooke, Michael (n.d.) 'Channel 4 and Film: How a Television Company Became a Major Film Industry Player', *Screenonline*. Online: http://www.screenonline.org.uk/film/id/1304135/index.html (accessed 1 November 2009).

Brown, Tom (2008) 'Spectacle/gender/history: The Case of *Gone with the Wind*', *Screen*, 49, 2, 157–78.

Brown, William (2009) 'Not Flagwaving but Flagdrowning, or Postcards from Post-Britain', in Robert Murphy (ed.) *The British Cinema Book*, 3rd edn. London: British Film Institute, 408–16.

Brunsdon, Charlotte (1990) 'Problems with quality', *Screen*, 31, 1, 67–90.

Brunt, Rosalind (1998) 'Icon' in 'Flowers and Tears: The Death of Diana, Princess of Wales', *Screen*, 39, 1, 68–70.

Bruzzi, Stella (1996 [1993]) 'Jane Campion: Costume Drama and Reclaiming Women's Past', in Pam Cook and Philip Dodd (eds) *Women and Film: A Sight and Sound Reader*. London: Scarlet Press, 232–42.

____ (1997) *Undressing Cinema: Clothing and Identity in the Movies*. London: Routledge.

Burdeau, Emmanuel (2006) 'Frears dans l'interrègne', *Cahiers du cinéma*, 616, 33–4.

Burgoyne, Robert (2008) *The Hollywood Historical Film*. Oxford: Blackwell.

Cardwell, Sarah (2002) *Adaptation Revisited: Television and the Classic Novel*. Manchester: Manchester University Press.

____ (2005) *Andrew Davies*. Manchester: Manchester University Press.

____ (2007) 'Is Quality Television Any Good?: Generic Distinctions, Evaluations and the Troubling Matter of Critical Judgement', in Janet McCabe and Kim Akass (eds) *Quality TV: Contemporary American Television and Beyond*. London: I.B. Tauris, 19–34.

Caughie, John (2000) *Television Drama: Realism, Modernism and British Culture*. Oxford: Oxford University Press.

Chapman, James (2005) *Past and Present: National Identity and the British Historical Film*. London: I.B. Tauris.

Choderlos de Laclos, Pierre (1961 [1782]) *Dangerous Liaisons*. Harmondsworth: Penguin.

Christie, Ian (2004) 'British Cinema: A View from (Elsewhere in) Europe', *Journal of British Cinema and Television*, 1, 1, 120–2.

Christopher, James (2006) 'Review of *The Queen*', *Times Online*, 14

September. Online: http://entertainment.timesonline.co.uk/tol/arts_ and_entertainment/film/film_reviews/article637978.ece (accessed 10 November 2009).

Chung, Hye Seung (2008) 'Reinventing the historical drama, de-westernizing a French classic: genre, gender, and the transnational imaginary in *Untold Scandal*', *Post Script*, 27, 3, 100–15.

Church Gibson, Pamela (2000) 'Fewer weddings and more funerals: changes in the Heritage Film', in Robert Murphy (ed.) *British Cinema of the 90s*. London: British Film Institute, 115–24.

____ (2002) 'From dancing queen to plaster virgin. *Elizabeth* and the end of English heritage?, *Journal of Popular British Cinema*, 5, 133–41.

Cook, Pam (1996) *Fashioning the Nation: Costume and Identity in British Cinema*. London: British Film Institute.

Corner, John and Sylvia Harvey (1991) 'Mediating tradition and modernity: the heritage/enterprise couplet', in John Corner and Sylvia Harvey (eds) *Enterprise and Heritage: Crosscurrents of National Culture*. London: Routledge, 45–75.

Cousins, Russell (1999) 'The Heritage Film and Cultural Politics: *Germinal* (Berri, 1993)', in Phil Powrie (ed.) *French Cinema in the 1990s: Continuity and Difference*. Oxford: Oxford University Press, 25–36.

Cox, Alex (2007) 'A Very British Cop-Out', *The Guardian*, 15 August. Online: http://film.guardian.co.uk/features/featurepages/0,,2149012,00.html (accessed 17 August 2007).

Craig, Cairns (2001 [1991]), 'Rooms without a View', in Ginette Vincendeau (ed.) *Film/Literature/Heritage: A Sight and Sound Reader*. London: British Film Institute, 3–6.

Cubitt, Sean (2005) *The Cinema Effect*. Cambridge, MA and London: MIT Press.

Custen, George F. (1992) *Bio/Pics: How Hollywood Constructed Public History*. Rutgers: New Brunswick.

Danan, Martine (1996) 'From a "Prenational" to a "Postnational" French Cinema', *Film History*, 8, 72–84.

Dave, Paul (1997) 'The Bourgeois Paradigm and Heritage Cinema', *New Left Review*, 224, 111–26.

Dawtrey, Adam (2008) 'A Crush of Queens Reign in a Celebrity Age', *Variety*, 409, 10, 19–21.

De Baecque, Antoine (1992) 'Le cinéma d'Europe à la recherche d'une forme', *Cahiers du cinéma*, 455/456, 78–84.

De Groot, Jerome (2009) *Consuming History: Historians and Heritage in Contemporary Popular Culture.* London: Routledge.

De la Bretèque, François (1992) 'Le film en costumes: un bon objet?', *Cinémaction*, 65, 111–22.

Duval, Roland (2007) 'De la "franchouillardise" dans le cinéma français', *Positif*, 557/558, 134–41.

Dyer, Richard (1994) 'Feeling English', *Sight and Sound*, 4, 3, 17–19.

_____ (1995) 'Heritage Cinema in Europe', in Ginette Vincendeau (ed.) *Encyclopaedia of European Cinema.* New York: Facts on File, 204–5.

_____ (2002) 'Homosexuality and Heritage', in *The Culture of Queers.* London: Routledge, 204–28.

_____ (2007) *Pastiche.* London: Routledge.

Edginton, Beth (1998) 'Nation', in 'Flowers and Tears: The Death of Diana, Princess of Wales', *Screen*, 39, 1, 79–81.

Ellis, John (1978) 'Art, Culture and Quality: Terms for a Cinema in the Forties and Seventies', *Screen*, 19, 3, 9–49.

_____ (1996) 'The Quality Film Adventure: British Critics and the Cinema, 1942–1948', in Andrew Higson (ed.) *Dissolving Views: Key Writings on British Cinema.* London: Cassell, 66–93.

Elsaesser, Thomas (1986) 'Film History as Social History: The Dieterle/Warner Brothers Bio-pic', *Wide Angle*, 8, 2, 15–31.

_____ (2005) *European Cinema: Face to Face with Hollywood.* Amsterdam: Amsterdam University Press.

_____ (2006 [1993]) 'Images for Sale: The "New" British Cinema', in Lester Friedman (ed.) *Fires Were Started: British Cinema and Thatcherism,* 2nd edn. London: Wallflower Press, 52–69.

Enns, Anthony (2007) 'The Politics of *Ostalgie*: Post-socialist Nostalgia in Recent German Film', *Screen*, 48, 4, 475–91.

Flaubert, Gustave (2003 [1857]) *Madame Bovary.* Harmondsworth: Penguin.

Fuller, Graham (2008) 'The Good Old Days', *Film Comment*, 44, 5, 36–8.

Funder, Anna (2007) 'Eyes Without a Face', *Sight and Sound*, 17, 5, 16–21.

Galt, Rosalind (2006) *The New European Cinema: Redrawing the Map.* New York: Columbia University Press.

Garrett, Roberta (1995) 'Costume Drama and Counter Memory: Sally Potter's *Orlando*', in Jane Dowson and Steven Earnshaw (eds) *Postmodern Subjects, Postmodern Texts.* Amsterdam: Rodopi, 89–99.

Gelder, Ken (1999) 'Jane Campion and the limits of literary cinema', in Deborah Carmell and Imelda Whelehan (eds) *Adaptations: From Text to Screen, Screen to Text.* London: Routledge, 157–71.

Geraghty, Christine (1998) 'Story', in 'Flowers and Tears: The death of Diana, Princess of Wales', *Screen*, 39, 1, 70–3.

___ (2000) 'Re-examining Stardom: Questions of Texts, Bodies and Performance', in Christine Gledhill and Linda Williams (eds) *Reinventing Film Studies.* London: Arnold, 183–201.

Gilbert, Sandra M. and Susan Gubar (1989) *No Man's Land: The Place of the Woman Writer in the Twentieth Century – Vol. 2: Sexchanges.* New Haven: Yale University Press.

Graham, Helen and Antonio Sánchez (1995) 'The Politics of 1992', in Helen Graham and Jo Labanyi (eds) *Spanish Cultural Studies: An Introduction – The Struggle for Modernity.* Oxford: Oxford University Press, 406–18.

Greene, Naomi (1999) *Landscapes of Loss: The National Past in Postwar French Cinema.* Princeton: Princeton University Press.

Griem, Julika and Eckart Voigts-Virchow (2002) 'Trashing and Recycling: Regenrification in British Heritage Movies and Costume Films of the 1990s', in Ewald Mengel, Hans-Jörg Schmid and Michael Steppat (eds) *Proceedings Anglistentag 2002 Bayreuth.* Trier: Wissenschaftlicher Verlag Trier, 319–31.

Grindon, Leger (1994) *Shadows in the Past: Studies in the Historical Fiction Film.* Philadelphia: Temple University Press.

Hall, Sheldon (2006) 'James Ivory (1928–)', in *Directors in British and Irish Cinema: A Reference Companion.* London: British Film Institute. Online: http://www.screenonline.org.uk/people/id/532213/index.html (accessed 1 November 2009).

___ (2009 [2001]) 'The Wrong Sort of Cinema: Refashioning the Heritage Film Debate', in Robert Murphy (ed.) *The British Cinema Book*, 3rd edn. London: British Film Institute, 46–56.

Halle, Randall (2002) 'German Film, *Aufgehoben*: Ensembles of Transnational Cinema', *New German Critique*, 87, 7–46.

Harper, Sue (1994) *Picturing the Past: The Rise and Fall of the British Costume Film.* London: British Film Institute.

___ (2004) 'The Taxonomy of a Genre: Historical, Costume and "Heritage" Film', *Journal of British Cinema and Television*, 1, 1, 137–42.

Hayward, Susan (2008) 'Reviewing Quality Cinema: French Costume Drama of the 1950s', *Studies in French Cinema*, 8, 3, 229–44.

Hewison, Robert (1987) *The Heritage Industry: Britain in a Climate of Decline*. London: Methuen.

Higson, Andrew (1995) *Waving the Flag: Constructing a National Cinema in Britain*. Oxford: Clarendon Press.

____ (1996) 'The Heritage Film and British Cinema', in Andrew Higson (ed.) *Dissolving Views: Key Writings on British Cinema*. London: Cassell, 232–48.

____ (2000) 'The Instability of the National', in Justine Ashby and Andrew Higson (eds) *British Cinema, Past and Present*. London: Routledge, 35–47.

____ (2003) *English Heritage, English Cinema: Costume Drama since 1980*. Oxford: Oxford University Press.

____ (2004) 'English Heritage, English Literature, English Cinema: Selling Jane Austen to Movie Audiences in the 1990s', in Eckart Voigts-Virchow (ed.) *Janespotting and Beyond: British Heritage Retrovisions Since the Mid-1990s*. Tübingen: Gunter Narr Verlag, 35–50.

____ (2006 [1993]) 'Re-presenting the National Past: Nostalgia and Pastiche in the Heritage Film', in Lester Friedman (ed.) *Fires Were Started: British Cinema and Thatcherism*, 2nd edn. London: Wallflower Press, 91–109.

Hill, John (1997) 'British Cinema as National Cinema: Production, Audience and Representation', in Robert Murphy (ed.) *The British Cinema Book*. London: British Film Institute, 244–54.

____ (1999) *British Cinema in the 1980s: Issues and Themes*. Oxford: Clarendon Press.

____ (2001) 'Contemporary British Cinema: Industry, Policy, Identity', *Cineaste*, 26, 4, 30–3.

Hipsky, Martin A. (1994) 'Anglophil(m)ia: why does America watch Merchant-Ivory movies?', *Journal of Popular Film and Television*, 22, 3, 98–107.

Hjort, Mette (2005) 'From Epiphanic Culture to Circulation: The Dynamics of Globalisation in Nordic Cinema', in Andrew Nestingen and Trevor G. Elkington (eds) *Transnational Cinema in a Global North*. Detroit: Wayne State University Press, 191–218.

____ (2010) 'On the Plurality of Cinematic Transnationalism', in Nataša Durovicová and Kathleen Newman (eds) *World Cinemas, Transnational Perspectives*. New York, Routledge, 12–33.

Hwang, Yun Mi (2011) 'South Korean *Sageuk*: History, Heritage and Cultural

Industry', Unpublished PhD thesis, Department of Film Studies, University of St Andrews, UK.

Iordanova, Dina (1999) 'East Europe's Cinema Industries Since 1989: Financing Structure and Studios', *The Public*, 6, 2, 45–60.

_____ (2003) *Cinema of the Other Europe: The Industry and Artistry of East Central European Film*. London: Wallflower Press.

Jäckel, Anne (2003) *European Film Industries*. London: British Film Institute.

_____ (2007) 'The Inter/Nationalism of French Film Policy', *Modern and Contemporary France*, 15, 1, 21–36.

James, Nick (2009) 'British Cinema's US Surrender – A View from 2001', in Robert Murphy (ed.) *The British Cinema Book*, 3rd edn. London: British Film Institute, 21–7.

Jameson, Fredric (1991) *Postmodernism, or, the Cultural Logic of Late Capitalism*. Durham: Duke University Press.

Johnston, Sheila (1985) 'Charioteers and Ploughmen', in Martin Auty and Nick Roddick (eds) *British Cinema Now*. London: British Film Institute, 99–110.

Jousse, Thierry (2000) 'L'habit ne fait past l'académisme', *Cahiers du cinéma*, 548, 42–3.

Judell, Brandon (2003) '"Girl with a Pearl Earring": Kate Hudson Walks, Vermeer Gawks, and Webber Talks. Interview with Peter Webber'. Online: http://www.indiewire.com/people/people_031218webber.html (accessed 11 May 2007).

Kemp, Philip (2006) 'Royal Blues', *Sight and Sound*, 16, 10, 28–30.

Kirschbaum, Erik (2005) 'New Wave of Euro Pix Avoids Europudding Curse', *Variety*, 31 October–6 November, 23–4.

Kitzinger, Jenny (1998) 'Image', in 'Flowers and Tears: the death of Diana, Princess of Wales', *Screen*, 39, 1, 73–9.

Klinger, Barbara (2006) 'The Art Film, Affect and the Female Viewer: *The Piano* Revisited', *Screen*, 47, 1, 19–41.

Koehler, Robert (2005) 'Speaking in Tongues: Entrants Reflect the Increasingly Multicultural Nature of Filmmaking Around the World', *Variety*, 19–25 December, A2.

Koepnick, Lutz (2002) 'Reframing the Past: Heritage Cinema and Holocaust in the 1990s', *New German Critique*, 87, 47–82.

Krewani, Angela (2004) 'Heritage as International Film Format', in Eckart

Voigts-Virchow (ed.) *Janespotting and Beyond: British Heritage Retrovisions since the Mid-1990s*. Tübingen: Gunter Narr Verlag, 161–6.

Leggott, James (2008) *Contemporary British Cinema: From Heritage to Horror*. London: Wallflower Press.

LeMahieu, D. L. (1990) 'Imagined Contemporaries: cinematic and televised dramas about the Edwardians in Great Britain and the United States, 1967–1985', *Historical Journal of Film, Radio and Television*, 10, 1, 243–56.

Luckett, Moya (2000) 'Image and Nation in 1990s British Cinema', in Robert Murphy (ed.) *British Cinema of the 1990s*. London: British Film Institute, 88–99.

Macnab, Geoffrey (2002) 'That shrinking feeling', *Sight and Sound*, 12, 10, 18–20.

_____ (2009) 'Eurimages plans contribution system restructure', *Screendaily*, 12 February. Online: http://www.screendaily.com/eurimages-plans-contribution-systemrestructure/4043269.article (accessed 26 July 2009).

Martin-Jones, David (2009) *Scotland: Global Cinema, Genres, Modes and Identities*. Edinburgh: Edinburgh University Press.

Mazierska, Ewa (2001) 'In the Land of Noble Knights and Mute Princesses: Polish Heritage Cinema', *Historical Journal of Film, Radio and Television*, 21, 2, 167–82.

McArthur, Colin (1982) 'Scotland and Cinema: The Iniquity of the Fathers', in Colin McArthur (ed.) *Scotch Reels: Scotland in Cinema and Television*. London: British Film Institute, 40–69.

McGowan, John (2000) 'Modernity and Culture, the Victorians and Cultural Studies', in John Kucich and Dianne F. Sadoff (eds) *Victorian Afterlife. Postmodern Culture Rewrites the Nineteenth Century*. Minneapolis: University of Minnesota Press, 3–28.

McKechnie, Kara (2001) 'Mrs Brown's Mourning and Mr King's Madness – Crisis in the Monarchy on Screen', in Imelda Whelehan, Deborah Cartmell and I. Q. Hunter (eds) *Retrovisions: Reinventing the Past*. London: Pluto Press, 102–19.

_____ (2002) 'Taking Liberties with the Monarch: The Royal Bio-pic in the 1990s', in Claire Monk and Amy Sargeant (eds) *British Historical Cinema*. London: Routledge, 217–36.

Moine, Raphaëlle and Pierre Beylot (2009), 'Introduction. Les fictions patrimoniales: une nouvelle catégorie interprétative', in Pierre Beylot and Raphaëlle Moine (eds) *Fictions patrimoniales sur grand et petit écran. Contours et enjeux d'un genre intermédiatique.* Bordeaux: Presses Universitaires de Bordeaux, 9–24.

Monk, Claire (1995) 'The British "Heritage Film" and its Critics', *Critical Survey*, 7, 2, 116–24.

_____ (2001 [1995]) 'Sexuality and Heritage', in Ginette Vincendeau (ed.) *Film/Literature/Heritage: A Sight and Sound Reader.* London: British Film Institute, 6–11.

_____ (2002) 'The British Heritage Film Debate Revisited', in Claire Monk and Amy Sargeant (eds) *British Historical Cinema.* London: Routledge, 176–98.

Murphy, Robert (2001) 'Introduction: British Cinema Saved - British Cinema Doomed', in Robert Murphy (ed.) *The British Cinema Book*, 2nd edn. London: British Film Institute, 1–7.

_____ (2009) 'Introduction', in Robert Murphy (ed.) *The British Cinema Book*, 3rd edn. London: British Film Institute, 1–2.

Napper, Lawrence (2000) 'British Cinema and the Middlebrow', in Justine Ashby and Andrew Higson (eds) *British Cinema, Past and Present.* London: Routledge, 110–23.

_____ (2009) *British Cinema and Middlebrow Culture in the Interwar Years.* Exeter: University of Exeter Press.

Neale, Steve (1986) 'Melodrama and Tears', *Screen*, 27, 6–23.

_____ (1990) 'Questions of Genre', *Screen*, 31, 1, 45–66.

Neely, Sarah (2005) 'Scotland, Heritage and Devolving British Cinema', *Screen*, 46, 2, 241–5.

Neiiendam, Jacob (2004) 'International Co-productions Face Funding Paradox', *Screendaily*, 4 March. Online: http://www.screendaily.com/ScreenDailyArticle.aspx?intStoryID=17639 (accessed 12 May 2007).

Nowell-Smith, Geoffrey (1997) *The Oxford History of World Cinema.* Oxford: Oxford University Press.

_____ (2004) 'Reflections on the European-ness, or Otherwise, of British Cinema', *Journal of British Cinema and Television*, 1, 1, 51–60.

Ostrowska, Dorota (2007) 'FRANCE: Cinematic Television or Televisual Cinema: INA and Canal+', in Dorota Ostrowska and Graham Roberts (eds) *European Cinemas in the Television Age.* Edinburgh: Edinburgh University Press, 25–40.

Ouditt, Sharon (1999) *'Orlando*: Coming Across the Divide', in Deborah Carmell and Imelda Whelehan (eds) *Adaptations: From Text to Screen, Screen to Text.* London: Routledge, 146–56.

Petley, Julian (1986) 'The Lost Continent', in Charles Barr (ed.) *All Our Yesterdays: 90 Years of British Cinema.* London: British Film Institute, 98–119.

Pidduck, Julianne (2004) *Contemporary Costume Film: Space, Place and the Past.* London: British Film Institute.

____ (2005) *La Reine Margot.* London: I.B. Tauris.

Pihama, Leonie (2000) 'Ebony and Ivory: Constructions of Maori in *The Piano*', in Harriet Margolis (ed.) *Jane Campion's The Piano.* Cambridge: Cambridge University Press, 114–34.

Pollock, Griselda (1980), 'Artists Mythologies and Media Genius, Madness and Art History', *Screen*, 21, 3, 57–96.

Powrie, Phil (1997) 'The Nostalgia Film', in *French Cinema in the 1980s: Nostalgia and the Crisis of Masculinity.* Oxford: Oxford University Press, 13–27.

____ (1999) 'Heritage, History and "New Realism": French Cinema in the 1990s', in Phil Powrie (ed.) *French Cinema in the 1990s: Continuity and Difference.* Oxford: Oxford University Press, 1–21.

Quart, Leonard (2006 [1993]) 'The Religion of the Market: Thatcherite Politics and the British Film of the 1980s', in Lester Friedman (ed.) *Fires Were Started: British Cinema and Thatcherism,* 2nd edn. London: Wallflower Press, 15–29.

Rivi, Luisa (2007) *European Cinema After 1989: Cultural Identity and Transnational Production.* New York: Palgrave Macmillan.

Roberts, Graham and Heather Wallis (2007), 'BRITAIN: Meet Mr Lucifer: British cinema under the spell of TV', in Dorota Ostrowska and Graham Roberts (eds) *European Cinemas in the Television Age.* Edinburgh: Edinburgh University Press, 6–24.

Roddick, Nick (2007) 'British cinema now: almost rosy', *Sight and Sound*, 17, 1, 22–4.

Rosenbaum, Jonathan (2001) 'Defenseless'. Review of *The Luzhin Defence* (Marleen Gorris, 2000). Online: http://www.jonathanrosenbaum.com/?s=luzhin+defence (accessed 29 May 2009).

Rosenstone, Robert (2007) 'In Praise of the Biopic', in Richard Francaviglia and Jerry Rodnitzky (eds) *Lights, Camera, History: Portraying the Past in*

Film. College Station: The University of Texas at Arlington, 11–29.

Sadoff, Dianne F. and John Kucich (2000) 'Introduction', in John Kucich and Dianne Sadoff (eds) *Victorian Afterlife: Postmodern Culture Rewrites the Nineteenth Century*. Minneapolis: University of Minnesota Press, ix–xxx.

Samuel, Raphael (1994) *Theatres of Memory, Vol. 1: Past and Present in Contemporary Culture*. London: Verso.

Sargeant, Amy (2000) 'Making and selling heritage culture: Style and authenticity in historical fictions on film and television', in Justine Ashby and Andrew Higson (eds) *British Cinema, Past and Present*. London: Routledge, 301–15.

Shakespeare, William (1995 [1597]) *King Henry IV: Part 1 and 2*. Buckingham: Open University Press.

Sonnett, Esther (1999) 'From *Emma* to *Clueless*: Taste, pleasure and the scene of history', in Deborah Carmell and Imelda Whelehan (eds) *Adaptations: From Text to Screen, Screen to Text*. London: Routledge, 51–62.

Sterne, Laurence (1983 [1759–67]) *The Life and Opinions of Tristram Shandy, Gentleman*. Oxford: Oxford University Press.

Stone, E. Kim (2004) 'Recovering the Lone Mother: *Howards End* as Aesthetic Anodyne', *Camera Obscura*, 55, 19, 1, 43–75.

Street, Sarah (2002) *Transatlantic Crossings: British Feature Films in the USA*. London: Continuum.

_____ (2004) '"The Mirror Crack'd": Heritage, History and Self-reflexive discourse', in Eckart Voigts-Virchow (ed.) *Janespotting and Beyond. British Heritage Retrovisions since the Mid-1990s*. Tübingen: Gunter Narr Verlag, 101–11.

Tashiro, C. S. (1998) *Pretty Pictures: Production Design and the History Film*. Austin: University of Texas Press.

Tasker, Yvonne and Diane Negra (2007) 'Introduction: Feminist Politics and Postfeminist Culture', in Yvonne Tasker and Diane Negra (eds) *Interrogating Postfeminism: Gender and the Politics of Popular Culture*. Durham: Duke University Press, 1–26.

Thabourey, Vincent (2005) 'Review of *Joyeux Noël*', *Positif*, 537, 59.

Truffaut, François (2009 [1954]) 'A Certain Tendency in French Cinema', in Peter Graham with Ginette Vincendeau (eds) *The French New Wave: Critical Landmarks*. London: British Film Institute, 39–63.

Urry, John (1990) *The Tourist Gaze: Leisure and Travel in Contemporary Society*. London: Sage.

Véray, Laurent (2009) '*Un long dimanche de fiançailles* et *Joyeux Noël*: patrimonialisation de la Grande Guerre come antidote aux angoisses mémorielles et à la déprime européenne', in Pierre Beylot and Raphaëlle Moine (eds) *Fictions patrimoniales sur grand et petit écran. Contours et enjeux d'un genre intermédiatique*. Presses Universitaires de Bordeaux, 153–66.

Vidal, Belén (2005) 'Playing in a Minor Key: The Literary Past Through the Feminist Imagination', in Mireia Aragay (ed.) *Books in Motion: Adaptation, Intertextuality, Authorship*. Amsterdam: Rodopi, 263–85.

____ (2007) 'Feminist Historiographies and the Woman Artist's Biopic: The Case of *Artemisia*', *Screen*, 48, 69–90.

Vincendeau, Ginette (1998) 'Issues in European Cinema', in John Hill and Pamela Church Gibson (eds) *The Oxford Guide to Film Studies*. Oxford: Oxford University Press, 440–8.

____ (2000) *Stars and Stardom in French Cinema*. London: Continuum.

____ (2001a) 'Introduction', in Ginette Vincendeau (ed.) *Film/Literature/Heritage. A Sight and Sound Reader*. London: British Film Institute, xi–xxxi.

____ (2001b [1995]), 'Unsettling Memories', in Ginette Vincendeau (ed.) *Film/Literature/Heritage: A Sight and Sound Reader*. London: British Film Institute, 27–32.

____ (2005) 'Un genre qui fait problème: le *Heritage film*. La critique face à un genre populaire des deux côtés de la Manche', in Raphaëlle Moine (ed.) *Le cinéma français face aux genres*. Paris: Association Française de Recherche sur l'Histoire du Cinéma, 131-140.

Voigts-Virchow, Eckart (2004) '"Corset Wars": An Introduction to Syncretic Heritage Film Culture since the Mid-1990s', in Eckart Voigts-Virchow (ed.) *Janespotting and Beyond: British Heritage Retrovisions Since the Mid-1990s*. Tübingen: Gunter Narr Verlag, 9–31.

Wayne, Mike (2001/2) 'The Re-invention of Tradition: British Cinema and International Image Markets', *EnterText*, 2, 1. Online: http://arts.brunel.ac.uk/gate/entertext/2_1_pdfs/wayne.pdf (accessed 10 November 2009).

____ (2002) *The Politics of Contemporary European Cinema: Histories, Borders, Diasporas*. Bristol: Intellect.

Wollen, Tana (1991) 'Over our shoulders: nostalgic screen fictions for the 1980s', in John Corner and Sylvia Harvey (eds) *Enterprise and Heritage: Crosscurrents of National Culture*. London: Routledge, 178–93.

Woolf, Virginia (1993 [1928]) *Orlando: A Biography*. Harmondsworth: Penguin.

Wright, Patrick (1985) *On Living in an Old Country: The National Past in Contemporary Britain*. London: Verso.

INDEX